Dave Hickey

Pirates and Farmers

PIRATES AND FARMERS

DAVE HICKEY

Ridinghouse

Well, my friends are gone and my hair is gray.
I ache in the places where I used to play.
And I'm crazy for love but I'm not coming on.
I'm just paying my rent every day in the Tower of Song.

Leonard Cohen, *Tower of Song*, 1988

For Jackie and Irving Blum

Contents

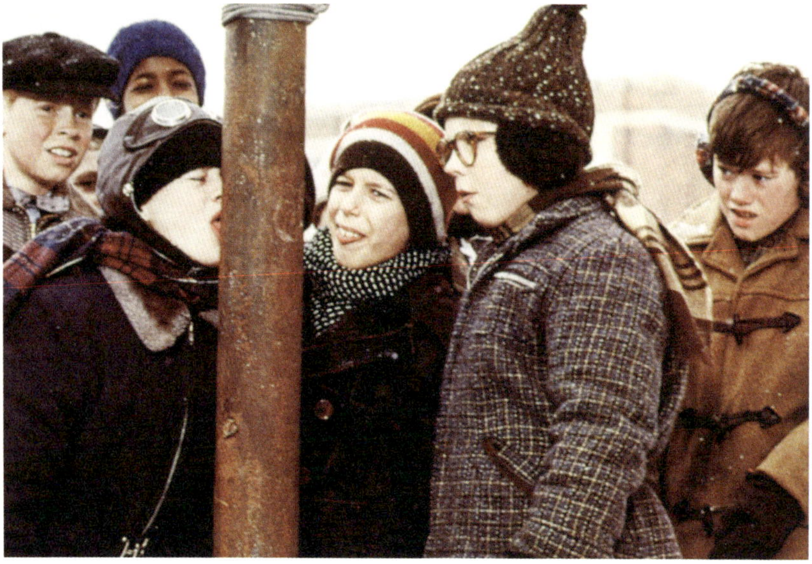

A Christmas Story, 1983
Film still

Introduction

On Taste

THERE are always absolutes. There are pirates and there are farmers. We are all one or the other, but even these genetic empires are scattered with protean archipelagos of taste. We want what we want, but like obsessive serial killers, we want it *exactly* the way we want it. We want the corpse wearing Mama's lipstick, so, along with aroma, taste is the oldest most precedent sense. Our lizard brains were tasting and smelling things long before we started worshipping them. So I should start with Andy Warhol, because his first masterpieces articulate the distinction between taste and desire.

In Warhol's radical democracy, the vitrine of high culture is a prison. There are desires endemic to the species that hold us together; there are shifting local tastes and traditions that keep us apart, and there are artists like Warhol whose ecumenical, global fame, *sans* vitrine, can unite the two. Warhol began with his soup-can paintings and his "Flavored Marilyns"—trademark desires produced in individual flavors to suit your taste. Everyone desires Campbell's Soup. It's the best stuff. Everybody desires Marilyn Monroe. She's the most desirable woman. But we all have our personal kinks, so Andy painted fifty-two Campbell soup-can paintings, each slightly different in its configuration and one painting for every flavor of soup: Cheese, Mushroom, Tomato, Clam Chowder, Bean and Bacon, etc. He painted about a dozen Flavored Marilyns—or Lifesaver Marilyns, as they were called at the Factory, since the candy provided the colors. All the Marilyns are identical in these paintings, but the backgrounds come in lime, orange, lemon, strawberry, pineapple, and licorice, to suit your taste while fulfilling your desires.

John Baldessari and I saw Andy's theory confirmed at a Warhol survey at the Whitney Museum of American Art. We were standing in a room hung with five large Electric Chair paintings in a variety of monochromes. A group of Park Avenue matrons strolled in, and without hesitation one of them said: "I like the blue one," and I could see her living room and imagine her childhood, the blue haze in her heart, and the grim pleasure she took in social executions. Standing there, I wondered, like Peggy Lee, "Is That All There Is?" because, as likely as not, that *is* all there is—not that there's anything wrong with that. My position is that ideology is fashion anyway, and for the last two centuries most of our bloody global comedies have begun with our inability to distinguish our desires from our tastes. It's hard to sort them out, but we know when they are not in tune.

When a virtue we recognize and believe in is too outré, we shamefully walk on by. On other occasions, we insist that our taste for cabbage and borscht and our preference for Nordic love goddesses constitute canonical cultural desires. This can have dire consequences. Tastes are fiercely held, protean, and invariably local. [Imagine Freud practicing in Rio.] Over the years, I have seen fistfights erupt in casino lounges over the relative quality of the whores at Soi Cowboy in Bangkok and the De Wallen whores in Amsterdam. I have seen skirmishes over the relative virtues of pickled herring and Japanese breakfast and over the relative manliness of fox hunting and baccarat. Duels have been fought over the silliness or sublimity of kilts, lederhosen, Mormon prairie dresses, and the teased silver hairdos of Southern dowagers.

James Madison actually argued for this distinction between taste and desire in the Tenth Federalist Paper. Since small republics are vulnerable to virulent faction, Madison suggested that this tendency would be mitigated in a large republic composed of multiple public proclivities, products, needs, climates, populations, and languages—multiple tastes but one desire: the maintenance of the republic. In Madison's view, the violence of local faction would be decontaminated by a commitment to the larger discourse of the liberal republic. In this way, an eighteenth-century savant, sitting at a polished desk in Montpelier, Virginia, formulated what physicists and climate scientists today call "hierarchical discontinuity"—the idea that a republic at ground level could be chaotic, complex, and rife with wind shear, yet still remain more checked and balanced at a national level, up above the clouds. As Peter Vierick argued in *Conservatism Revisited*, even conservatives are trying to conserve a liberal democracy. Otherwise they're treacherous radicals.[1]

This distinction is a consummation much to be desired in a commercial republic. The lesson for art mavens today is that the art business continues but, up in the stratosphere, its vitrine of exclusivity has evanesced. Art is irrelevant. The newsworthy transformations wrought by Picasso, Pollock, Warhol, and Robert Mapplethorpe have been replaced by shiny ghosts. They are not news, and they are not new. Some work is just more recent. The last "new" thing I saw was break dancing. Our museum exhibitions—like the art in collectors' summer homes—are "group shows" held together by the most banal feature of the works on display and by the majesty of undifferentiated diversity. It's hard to mount a one-person exhibition and still be fair and maintain that multifaceted mediocrity that keeps one's enemies at bay.

Art, in live culture, however, out in the scumbled street is the wild card in the hand that culture deals us—the talisman that gives us back something we have just lost or just started wanting. It completes the hand we hold, or would if there were sufficient wild cards on display. There are not, so I just live with the fact that the biker next door is a Nazi. Okay, Bobby Joe is a Nazi. The fact that he can go inside, open his computer with the swastika decal and communicate with every other Nazi in the world is unnerving, but that's life in the Global Village.

What comforts me is the thought of Billy Joe, Anders Behring Breivik, assorted Croatians, and the shallow end of Reinhard Heydrich's gene pool all assembled in Texas Stadium in Dallas. The odds against all these bikers, skinheads, twee barons, soccer thugs, ethnic cleansers, and Wall Street wolverines, standing in uniformed ranks and simultaneously saluting in the proper manner, are beyond computation. There would be wrangling over precedence, form, and apparel. Fights would start. Shooting would begin. Everyone would battle for their own flavor of Hitler soup and their own Hitler-flavored Lifesaver, and we could watch this nouveau "Night of the Long Knives" on cable news. This is life in the global village, too.

This would confirm my long-held suspicion that cosmopolitan cultures are like teenage bands. They only come together so they can fall apart, and we can cherish our memories of The Lavender Guppies in their halcyon days, and the craziness of Siegfried in its heavy-metal majesty. Try to stage a reunion and all the shit comes flooding back. So this book is not about art that is on sale or on display. It is about the art we *choose*, and having chosen, choose to keep: good art, bad art, fine art, folk art, ad art, and fashion art, whichever presents itself. Art that exists in the world, in the possession of civilians, is the accumulated hard copy of cosmopolitanism and civilization. It's all in what we choose and not in what we would or could or should. Any founder of this republic would assure you that it takes a village to make a tyranny, and it all starts with mandatory borscht, Japanese breakfast, desert-tan lipstick, and becoming "judgmental" about boobies. We all have our tongues stuck to the frozen flagpole. Taste rolls on like the gigantic waves in the Roaring Forties. Desire, like Faulkner's Dilsey, endures.

1 Peter Viereck, *Conservatism Revisited*, Collier Macmillan, New York, 1962.

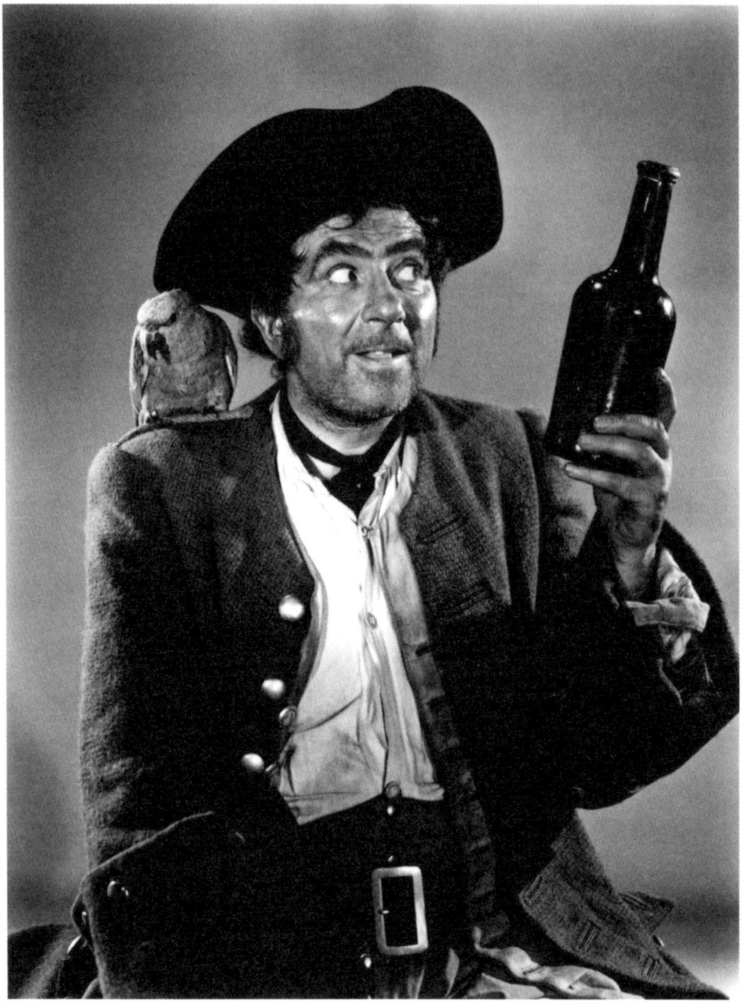

Robert Newton in *Blackbeard the Pirate*, 1952
Film still

Pirates and Farmers

I AM going to explain this to you very simply. All human creatures are divided into two groups. There are pirates, and there are farmers. Farmers build fences and control territory. Pirates tear down fences and cross borders. There are good pirates and bad pirates, good farmers and bad farmers, but there are *only* pirates and farmers. They are very different kinds of creatures, and some pirates even recognize the importance of farmers. My late friend Roger Miller, a famous pirate, wrote this in a song after a visit with his tax attorney, "Squares make the world go round," he wrote, "Sounds profane sounds profound/But Government things can't be made do/ By hipsters wearin' rope-soled shoes."

Farmers, on the other hand, *always* hate pirates. What's more, farmers always *recognize* pirates even when the pirate being recognized has yet to recognize him or herself as a pirate. One of the ways that pirates come to recognize themselves as pirates is through the experience of being recognized and persecuted by farmers. There are many unaware pirates, however, in workplaces around the world, who wonder why they are never invited to the weenie roast. They are pirates, but they just don't know, and you should know who you are before you turn forty-five, buy an assault weapon, and wipe out a nursing college.

So you should try some things out. Enter the territory of some farmer-friendly enterprise, like the Department of Motor Vehicles, or the student union at the University of Alabama, or the boardroom of AIG. If everyone glares at you sullenly and touches their wallet pocket, you may be a pirate. If you think you're a pirate, ablaze with exasperation, you probably are, but you should research further. Commit some petty offenses: park in a handicapped zone, jaywalk, refuse to return the attached form in triplicate, or just take an Incomplete in Hegel and His Times, and then never write the paper.

If these transgressions don't get your panties in a bunch, it's a pirate's life for you. Embrace your moment of self-awareness and get on with life. You are not the *only* pirate in the world, and remember this: *pirates are born and not made*. It's not something your mother did to you. It's not something the government did to you or any of those amazing things Counselor Rick did to you in the shower at summer camp. You were *born* a pirate! Raise that skull and crossbones! Sail away!

Never forget that one of the chief causes of personal unhappiness in the US of A, where farmer culture is all but hegemonic, is the denial of pirate identity, because farmers always know who's a pirate. Pirates don't always know what they are. Very often the children of pirates, who are in fact pirates them-selves, seek to deny their piratical natures and pass as farmers in order to rebel against their pirate parents. This rarely works out well in the long run, but sometimes it does. Take the case of Melinda, an accidental recidivist. She grew up during the 1950s in a pirate family of hard-line communists. As a consequence, Melinda grew up hating Communism, which she associated with people smoking cigars and shouting about Fascism in the kitchen while Aunt Tilly played old 78s of Mahler symphonies at top volume on the phonograph. Melinda wanted to play Ruth Brown and The Clovers but there was no help for it. These circumstances led Melinda to associate being a pirate with being a communist.

So Melinda resolved to become a farmer. In her sophomore year at Berkeley, she met a young man from Wisconsin who had renamed himself Earth Free. He wanted to be a farmer, too, so they moved to Oregon to be farmers together. Fortunately, they almost immediately came upon a commune called Free Earth. They took this as a sign and joined forthwith. Here they lived happily in a derelict school bus. They smoked marijuana cigarettes, had group sex, and did very little farming at all. In this way, by virtual happenstance, Melinda's pirate nature was able to reassert itself. Things did not turn out so well, however, for Melinda's daughter J. L. [Janis Lives]. Having grown up naked and dirty in a bus, sorting seeds and stems, and listening to Electric Flag and Canned Heat, J. L. came to associate being a pirate with being a hippie, and she really hated hippies.

Thus it was, when J. L. herself finally matriculated at Berkeley, she immediately became a communist. Unfortunately, the communists she fell in with were not *pirate* communists, they were *farmer* communists—tenured communists with an infrastructure of ideological imperatives and dietary laws that made an orthodox Shiite festival look like a Flaming Lips concert. Almost immediately J. L. was caught smoking. Then, not long thereafter, in rebellion against a childhood of tofu and sprouts, she was observed scarfing down a Big Mac. From there, it was only a short step to the ideological heresy that got her ostracized. This involved a sex act employing an object that could only serve to perpetuate the commodity fetishism of late-capitalist culture. Today, J. L. works as a dental assistant in Encinitas, where she is not a happy camper.

This demonstrates a common fallacy: that of associating the eternal distinction between pirates and farmers with the petty local fashions that define political and cultural ideologies in the twentieth century. We can't be any firmer on this point.

There are right-wing pirates and left-wing pirates; there are right-wing farmers and left-wing farmers, but there are *only* pirates and farmers. The good thing about farming is that it keeps you busy at home and pays steady subsidies. The good thing about piracy is that it is cosmopolitan; you get to move around, and when it pays at all it pays *very well*. This might seem a fair enough trade-off, but it often spells doom for extremely competent pirates who, having amassed mountain ranges of Spanish doubloons, gold bullion, jewelry, and brass cannons find themselves feeling peckish and down in the mouth from all the rushing about that is intrinsic to the pirate lifestyle. They find themselves, say, driving down US40 through Arkansas with their pirate crew. Glancing over to the side of the road, they see a beautiful horse farm with white fences and green pastures full of elegant thoroughbreds. The animals' sleek coats are gleaming in the sun. Pristine, white, colonial-style stables, with cupolas and weather vanes blaze like a dream of Monticello and, way back there among the trees, at the top of a circular drive, they glimpse an antebellum mansion.

Seeing all this, the successful pirate remarks to his pirate crew: "I've worked damned hard at piracy, you know, and worked damned long. I've raped, pillaged, plundered, and sent many a king's man to a watery grave. The wake behind my schooner has looped the world a hundred times. So why shouldn't I seek a bit of refuge and respite. Why shouldn't I retire to a horse farm just like this? I have enough hard capital to buy this damn farm with the rings on my right hand."

Herein resides the paradox of pirate retirement. You can't do it. Piracy is a genetic proclivity. You strap on your peg leg, don your eye patch, take a swig of rum, and die at the helm or by the blade, or you end up destitute in Port Royale, sitting on the dock of the bay. At this point in the captain's reverie, one hopes that the successful pirate's hearty comrades will speak up firmly. Honoring the tradition of pirate democracy, they will say:

Your pirates ain't your farmers, Cap'n Jack. Farmers *hate* pirates something fierce, and even if you buy a farm, consort with farm animals, and wear a farmer hat, they will know you for a pirate. They will mobilize and take action, and what do pirates know of farmer fighting—of farmer martial arts—of water districting, tax assessing, zoning, easements, and such? What pirate with a single *cojone* knows dick about subcontractors, plumbing contractors, or any other kind of contractor? About condemnations, imminent domain, and rights of way? To be honest, Cap'n, your forthright pirate way of fighting would be naught but child's play to them. They would run you down in the road, steal you blind, sue you till your toes hurt, and, worst of all, *you could not sail away*! You would just be there, becalmed on this farm in the middle of nowhere, and even if you overcame all these obstacles through the auspices of a corrupt farmer lawyer, you know what they would do? They would shoot your dog and burn your horses in their stalls.

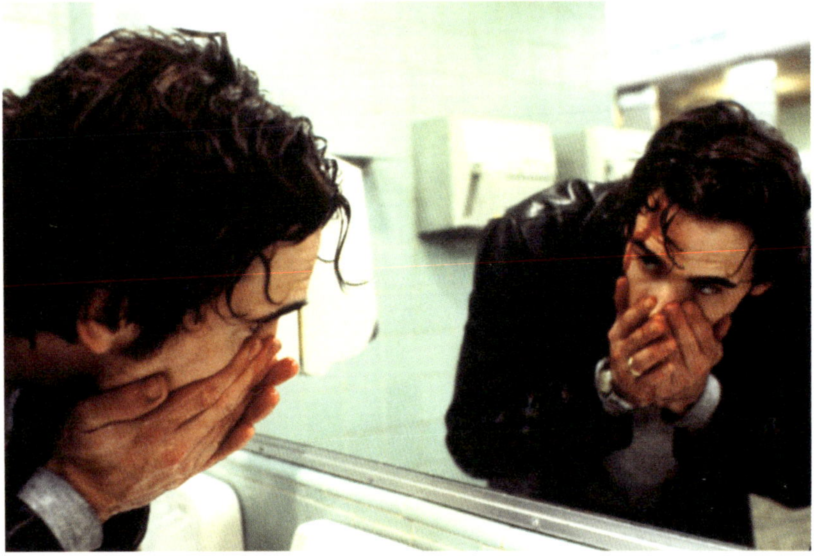

Matt Dillon in *Drugstore Cowboy*, 1989
Film still

The Weather Outside

It's something how the life will fall as to how the heart is tossed.
JOHN STEWART, *The Eyes of Sweet Virginia*, 1982

AT THE age of eleven, with no drama whatsoever, I moved out of my mother's house, and for the next thirty-five years I traveled, wrote, and did a lot of drugs. Everyone told me that I would die, but I didn't. Today, to paraphrase Professor Harold Hill in *The Music Man*, the hours I've spent with a straw up my nose are gold. As a true citizen of the dark side, I have experienced most varieties of pleasure and pain in the company of other shitbags and drugged-out rock-and-roll trash like myself. I hung out at Andy's Factory and Norman Fisher's penthouse. I hitched rides on private planes flying north from southern Mexico, wobbly with bales of weed and beer coolers packed with contraband Mayan cylinders and Styrofoam peanuts. I shot up speedballs in the restroom of an evangelist's private jet in the skies over Ohio. I chatted over coffee in the zócolo in Toluca with a big pistol tucked in my pants. I relaxed on a lumpy couch in a tweeker double-wide with an Uzi on the gray enamel coffee table. I rode along on late-night adventures with Allen Toussaint, Waylon Jennings, Butch Trucks, Lowell George, and a host of other transient luminaries. In one hazy, addled sequence that resembled nothing so much as the movie Groundhog Day for schizophrenics, I covered Aerosmith's *Rocks* tour, a New York Dolls reunion in Detroit, Lou Reed's *Rock 'n' Roll Animal* tour, and Lynyrd Skynyrd's *Gimme Back My Bullets* tour—not one of which I could have survived without drugs and a very high shame threshold.

I covered Gregg Allman's drug trial in Macon for *The Village Voice*, on drugs, of course, because Dickey Betts, seeking my sympathy, pulled out the quart-size baggie he kept folded in his boot. I also rode shotgun [with a shotgun] for a friend who scored four pounds of meth in a goat shed amidst the human infestation that nestles around the south end of the Salton Sea. I fell down a rain-slick mountain in Peru, and Billy Joe Shaver fell down on top of me. I stammered through a queasy morning in my mother's perfect living room with two smooth ATF agents who appeared at the door. They were interested in my college roommate. They wondered why my phone number kept showing up on their phone trap. I thanked whatever gods-may-be that it was a trap and not a tap because [master criminals that we were] I routinely called up to order "two ounces of Jethro Tull albums." Once, in desperation, disconnected in Atlanta, I paid top dollar for an ounce of Vitamin B6. Once, in a motel on the Sunset Strip, I tried to fuck a nubile starlet who was anxious to fuck journalists from national magazines. I failed in this endeavor because the drugs that provided me with the panache to try denied me the ability to perform. I resolved the situation to the taste of blueberry bodywash and told everybody that I banged her brains out. Boogie nights.

A few blocks down the Sunset Strip, and fifteen floors above it, I sat on one of those concrete slabs that used to extend from rooms on the front of the Hyatt to block out the lights of the Strip. I enjoyed the view, relished the vertigo, and listened attentively to a Valley Girl, who was deconstructing the nuances of Jimmy

Page's relationship with the occult. A few days later, in Montecito, staying at a friend's house, I drifted off for a little nap and woke up under a sky full of stars, in a spa full of blood-red bubbles. My friend threatened to charge me for spa maintenance. I went back to New York and prepared for my first [and only] appearance on Bill Buckley's *Firing Line* by spending the night before coked up and naked in a sauna with twin Filipino fashion models. Excepting girls with multiple personalities, this was one of my two experiences with group sex [if twins count as a group], and it was not too bad. My performance as adjunct art expert on *Firing Line*, however, sucked bears.

I called these stupid stunts adventures, and in those years, I was all about adventures. For you, with your trust fund, your loft and your driver, your group interventions, and safety nets, they may seem tawdry. For me, they were magical, raggedy, and legion. I could get paid to go anywhere to look at anything and write about it because I was a good slick magazine writer and relatively punctual. I caught the shiniest train that came by and disembarked at the first glimmer of ennui to catch another. Sadly, the rising arc of excess began to flatten in the 1980s. I was stranded in Fort Worth while my mother was furiously dying, and one morning I noticed that X, one of my favorite bands, was playing in a club called Zero's. When X played Zero's, I felt my attendance was required. I wore a black Kinks ball cap and a long cowboy duster, and I leaned against the back wall. Except for Exene and the rest of the band, I was twenty years older than anyone else in the room. That was fine with me until an acne-challenged youth walked up and asked politely, "Do you have any Quaaludes, sir?" It occurred to me then that there might be an expiration date on stupid adventures, and there was, although I spent another decade in denial.

Then drugs killed all my friends and made my face fall off. My friends chose their own paths, of course, but losing whatever beauty I had was a blow. [I mean, seriously, would you rather be ugly or dead?] As this point, I was living in a second-floor studio in Ocean Beach overlooking the Pacific. In my solitude, I quickly realized that when all one's friends are dead, the peer pressure is zip. But I still didn't quit drugs. Not in my mind. I went on hiatus. I didn't go to meetings or pray or anything like that. I just started paying my bills on time and held on tight. I kept smoking cigarettes and betting on professional basketball down at the Pacific Shores. I marched down Newport Avenue in the Frosty Parade for aging surfers. I ran up and down the hills above the beach, wasting an hour a day for a high I could have gotten with one line of Peruvian flake. I also did my part for the cause. A thrasher band rehearsed in the bungalow next door, and after an afternoon of pitiful cacophony, I walked over, politely introduced myself, and showed them the chords to "Wild Thing." [There aren't too many.]

During this period, I felt better and slept better, *but I was trapped in the fucking middle class*! No more Uzis or boobalicious starlets. The magical Teflon shield that had always separated me from the straight world had evanesced, and there I was. I had always lived amid that world, of course, but I was never a part of it. Other people loaned me their clubs and signed my chit at the Nineteenth Hole. Now, I was wearing my tuxedo to museum openings, lecturing at universities, chatting up remittance men in La Jolla, and going to dinner parties with snot-bubbling babies in attendance, coming home at 9.30pm. In this milieu, I quickly realized that my friends who professed to have "problems" with drugs, really had a problem with the degree to which using and trafficking in drugs excludes one from this bourgeois paradise, and I felt betrayed. Somehow, I had made it through fifty years without living in the middle class. My folks were outsiders. My friends were artists, writers, musicians, art dealers, and criminals. We were right about the middle class. It sucks.

I learned other things during my hiatus—not as much as I learned from lesbian strippers, as we gobbled hot tapas on Paradise Boulevard in Las Vegas, but valuable lessons nevertheless. For thirty years, careening through Adventureland, I assiduously maintained the business of writing for deadlines. It was my solitary discipline, and a real one. The night after the morning my mother died, I scored some crank and wrote a 6,000-word piece about Hank Williams—because I said I would—while my brother and sister were downstairs plundering my mother's possessions. Now I discovered, to my vast disappointment, that I did not need drugs to write—that I *wanted* drugs to write because I wanted dessert first. Then, on a long California afternoon, I used the time I was saving by living the straight life to read through the clips of my own writing that I had around the apartment. There were not too many, because pirates, as a rule, squander the treasure and treasure the blame. I don't have, like, a file of writing, as Don DeLillo does, but there were enough pieces laying around in yellowed magazines to demonstrate that the writing I wrote straight and the writing I wrote with my consciousness altered by acid, speed, coke, booze, smack, and barbiturates did not differ in any significant way.

So maybe writing wasn't about consciousness at all. Maybe it was a birth defect in the lizard brain and a much more mysterious activity than I had ever imagined. Then I realized that I was actually "talented"—in the sense that writing was easy and fun for me and always had been. In the sense that straight or bent, in high spirits or low, in fame and ignominy, I have always been ravished by writing about the spectacle of the visible world. I love writing and the sunshine on the wall, and, realizing this, I could see that my long procession of drama-queen deadline crises had arisen from some vestigial, Calvinist presumption that writing was hard. Somehow, I thought you had to pay to be a writer. You don't, but I wanted people to think that I was suffering. I realize now, of course, that nature blessed (or damned) me with a sharp tongue and a critical intelligence well above my station, and that being stoned, or appearing to be stoned, somehow ameliorated the outrageous things I said and did. Some people get stoned to get smart. I did it to get stupid because I am a very diverse person. To fit in among the margins of the chosen, I addled my brain, the way that Tim Duncan, while growing up to his seven feet of basketball genius, developed a stoop while maturing among tiny people in the Virgin Islands.

Other revelations bordered on the infantile. For thirty years, I stayed up all night to write. From nine in the evening until three in the morning, I listened to music, popped pills, snorted powders, and read John Ruskin. At 3am, I would start writing and write for about six hours; then I would walk down to the Little Chef for gyros and eggs at the beach. Then one day, it came to me. Why not take a *nap* from nine till three? And then get up and write! And, it worked! My production went up by a third, and all I missed was reading Ruskin while the palms clattered in the breeze—and, truly, a little bump enhances reading Ruskin. Ray Carver wrote *stories* shorter than some of Ruskin's paragraphs. There were other small downsides. Liberated from the expense of drugs and factoring in my enhanced production, I found myself with money in the bank. Since I only write for money, money in the bank made me feel lazy. I thought, for the briefest instant, about going back to surfing, but surfing in Ocean Beach at that time was the province of 'roid-rage' gangbangers in wet suits. So I watched *Perry Mason*, ate take-out Chinese, read Robert Browning and Julio Cortázar, and became terminally bored with my petit-bourgeois existence.

I solved all this by moving to Las Vegas, where you are never alone with your devils or angels—where there are virtually no Protestants, a surfeit of gaming opportunities, and a cornucopia of louche citizens wise in the realm of statistics, obeisant to the law of large numbers. In most of America, one is presumed straight and must prove oneself otherwise. This gets to be a chore. In Vegas [as in rock and roll], one is presumed fucked from jump. No explanation or acting out required. Best of all, a sixty-something white guy in sweatpants, a T-shirt, and a ball cap disappears into Vegas like sand into the desert. So I expanded my gambling habit to fill the void left by my drug habit, and since gambling and drugs are contraindicated, it worked. As Lord Byron noted, gambling has the virtues of wine and women but you can do it longer—longer at a time and further into in your maturity.

I also discovered the advantage of gambling over cocaine. I never did a line of blow after which some guy burst in the door and shouted, "You just won twenty more lines!" Otherwise it was all there, the adrenaline, the shallow sociability, the ultimate, potentially catastrophic seriousness of what you are risking, and the sublime oblivion of being delivered into the moment. Two years of Texas Hold 'em, however, taught me something about the nature of my own competitiveness. I *love* to win, but I don't really like to *beat* people, and nontournament Hold 'em, as it is played in Las Vegas casinos, is mostly a matter of raptors who want to win by taking money away from herbivores who are happy to lose if they can just sit at the table. Once I figured this out, it stopped being fun. If people don't mind if they are losing or if they want to lose or *need* to lose, you're not actually winning. The heavens are not as well aligned as they might seem.

So I quit Hold 'em—sadly, because it is a beautiful game, and happily too because I don't naturally, in writing or cards, compete against my peers. I am a fucking radical. I compete against the House, the Institution, the University, and the Church, always. I want the House brought down. I want love among the ruins and, even though I can't achieve this fantasy, I can still deploy my foxiness against the House's edge and relish my little victories—in cards as I do in writing. When the odds of my beating the House in writing surpassed the odds of my beating the House at cards, my gambling became less feverish. Today it is a private refuge where I may, as often as I wish, for as long as I want, luxuriate in the great, brave drift of an America you never heard of.

I can imagine you now, shaking your heads in pity, so be assured that I don't care what you think. There is nothing in the Constitution that says you can't be who you are—that you can't live or die with the consequences of that. The bet you make by cultural compliance [of being accepted, secure, praised, and living forever] is not a good bet, particularly if you are who I am. So this is my version of the psychological facts: First, genetics matter, a lot, as does the shape of the negative space in your heart. Second, what tickles your fancy kills your friends, so dead friends come with the territory. Third, chaotic childhoods endow us with attributes that are useful for artists and writers and gamblers. They make us hyper-attentive to the world around us. They allow us insight into the benign details of dress and behavior that might foreshadow immediate catastrophe. So we are cagey. We know that it's always brightest just before it goes completely black.

In this sense, our personalities are *designed* for chaos. We are predisposed to and prepared for creative activity. Unfortunately, creative activity, good or bad, doesn't cure anything, ever. Therapy might help, but I've never tried it. Drugs and gambling are provisional forms of maintenance, which is nice, because most of us are not looking for a cure. Some of us have grown up amid chaos and have taken to it. Coping with disaster is what we do, so we walk the edge of the cliff. Society can do without us, but the species requires our presence. The species needs people who don't give a fuck what you think, who are predisposed to tell the truth, ride the tiger, and jump on the grenade. More specifically, the species needs people who are *good* at this sort of thing, who have *practiced*. So, I'm up for it when it all comes down. Sometimes, however, when my bones creak as I rise from the card table, I fear that I may have over-trained for the reckoning.

Idiot

MY DOWNWARD spiral into idiocy began when I agreed to curate a biennial exhibition at SITE Santa Fe in 2001. The process turned out to be an unremitting nightmare, mitigated by hiccups of ecstasy. I took the job on a lark. Five minutes in, I realized that my primary agenda would be to save as much face as I had left. So I paid people who didn't work. I worked people I couldn't pay. I was often at the ATM withdrawing chunks of my fee because in the State of New Mexico one is expected to tip work crews and regional art centers do not. So I doled out tips and fielded calls from functionaries in Scandinavia, Asia, Central Europe, and the Middle East. They offered to fly me business class to their native lands, put me up in hotel rooms with balconies, and provide drivers for my tours of government-approved art. I politely declined these junkets. Curators, being certified sleazebags, may do this sort of thing; art critics may not—because it's not right.

A week before my show opened, I nearly tipped over from cardiac arrhythmia. I drove myself to a clinic. A doctor from Mumbai bopped me with a Valium drip and gave me some pills that, he promised, would postpone my demise. I soldiered on. We opened the show, and it was cool. Of all the biennials I have ever walked through, I liked walking through mine the best.

I had saved face to my own satisfaction. I had survived. I had been there and done that, and a month later, I received an invitation to a conference in Spain titled "A Biennale of Biennales"—a cruel joke, I suspected, designed to escalate my daily dose of Amiodarone, but no. It was an actual event. All the "really big" biennial curators would be there having meetings. I convulsively declined. Not long thereafter, Robert Hughes was invited to curate the 2005 Venice Biennale. This sounded like good, dirty fun, but Bob declined almost immediately. He could not, he said, "countenance ditherers."

Then I went totally idiot. *Hey*, I thought, *I've done a biennial! I have the skill set. Maybe* I *could do a Venice Biennale!* The art would be easy since there's only so much, and it would be so cool, I thought, to be in Venice in the winter, when the fog is down and the water is up over the walkways, where it feels like old, cold Venice as you slog along, pushing black waves before you, expecting some dude in an opera cape and a plague mask to jump out, stick a dagger in your tummy and float you off down the Grand Canal. Oh boy! I began conjuring cool ideas for double-decking the Arsenale so it looked like a shopping mall. I decided that, in my biennial, no work of art would be bigger than a Shetland pony. I decided that I would not commission installations sight unseen. That is patronage, not curating, and it's not right either.

I imagined a travel budget as big as the Doge's Palace. I dreamed of North Africa with its blinding sunshine, black shadows, and heroic hashish. I thought about Raffles in Singapore, the casinos in Macao, and the sex boîtes of Bangkok, where they serve you Viagra with your Mekong whiskey. I thought about the Happy Valley Racecourse in Hong Kong, plopped down in its nest of glass skyscrapers, awash with the perfume of horseshit and fresh-cut grass, glistening with thoroughbreds and the elegance of flamingos. I thought about the surf outside of Brisbane. Maybe I would chase down the guy who did the video of the bikini girls chain-sawing surfboards in a beach hotel room.

I toyed with the idea of taking Rauschenberg's advice and doing a show of art between the tropics to avoid packing winter clothing—or maybe I would hire some equatorial beauty for whom the ice and snow would be exotic. She could do the cold parts. Then I could visit Mutt-Mutt in New Orleans and check out his new Mardi Gras feathers. I could visit the coffin dudes of Accra. I could hang with Kwame Akoto, the self-proclaimed Almighty God, in Kumasi. I could sweat, drink local beer, and slap bugs. Then I could hurry back to slurpy, noir Venice to plot out small salons, modest atriums, and parades of Palladian doorways.

I refined these daydreams until Rosa Martínez and María de Corral were appointed to curate the 2005 Venice Biennale. Then, before I could get my reverie cranked up again, my friend Robert Storr was appointed to curate the 2007 Biennale. Martínez had curated the Santa Fe Biennial before mine. Storr had curated the Santa Fe Biennial after mine. Had I schlepped to Spain to dine with people whose taste I don't respect, I would have been miffed, but rejection is a big part of a writer's life. In any case, my wife and I alternate Venice Biennales, so Libby and all her shoes visited the 2005 de Corral-Martínez edition. Her report on the outcome was guarded, although she had a great Barbara Gladstone story.

Rob Storr's 2007 edition in Venice was immaculate and enormously enhanced by the premiere showing of Yang Fudong's *Seven Intellectuals in a Bamboo Forest* [2003–07] in all five of its parts. Unlike most biennial art, Yang Fudong's films transcend race, region, gender, culture, and tedium. They are all about art. [What a concept!] With these films as its centerpiece, Storr's Venice Biennale was astringent and refreshing. The art was too big, of course—*way* too big. There were too many brains and skulls for my taste, but, even so, the pervasive ambience of clean melancholia was a welcome relief from the thrift-shop fecklessness of most recent biennials. The bleakness made Storr's exhibition feel more like an auteurist production than he said he intended it to be, but I found no fault in that. My own exhibitions are always deemed to be more ebullient than is proper, and it's not like there's an International Mood Code that one mustn't violate. So Storr's show wasn't me, but, hey, if I wanted me, I could have stayed at home and looked at my own art.

On the flight back, I read Storr's introductory catalogue essay instead of Robbe-Grillet in French, my favorite airplane reading. Storr's tone was as winsome and nonconfrontational as a dozing puppy. I wondered about that until I read the reviews. There were a lot of them. Most of them were very unkind. Yang Fudong was not discussed. *Artforum* published a quartet of volleys by Okwui Enwezor, Jessica Morgan, Francesco Bonami, and Katy Siegel. Katy and I are mere art critics, so we saw the same show. Enwezor, Morgan, and Bonami clearly think of themselves as "biennial critics"—Knights Templar guarding the bloodless grail. They addressed the exhibition as NASA bureaucrats might review the latest shuttle launch while auditioning to direct the next. If Storr's essay was a snoozing puppy, the "reviews" were so feline I felt like my beagle, Ralph, straining at the leash, because thirty years in the art world and hundreds of biennials had not prepared me for the unctuous, trivial world these texts revealed: the conferences, committees, agendas, proposals, symposia, position papers, tourist boards, petty quarrels, prize adjudications, directorial appointments, and preening philanthropists. Imagine Lewis Carroll on bad acid. Oh my.

Enwezor's review begins with shamanistic foreboding. He evokes the collective unconsciousness of his cult by employing the passive voice in its most aggressive mode. "Even before the gates of the Giardini opened," Enwezor confides, "an unspoken sense of doom and boredom seemed to have set in." Then, one paragraph thereafter, Enwezor glances down from his pedestal to inform any high-school dropout reading *Artforum* at the orthodontist's office that the term "cultural production" may be attributed to the French sociologist Pierre Bourdieu—*quel surprise*, you silly fuck! Thenceforth, flickering between the poles of narcissistic erudition and global omniscience, Enwezor, Morgan, and Bonami impugn Storr's character, his qualifications, worldliness, politics, taste, track record, American heritage, and general worthiness to carry on "the kind of curatorial irreverence and ingenuity that transformed the art world in 1990s into a truly global affair." One could only assume that Storr had broken some solemn oath to perpetuate clusterfuck curating. If so, good for him.

When the assassination was over, I had to smile. In my ruthless, little, adversarial business, the disapprobation of swanning poseurs is much to be desired, so I felt good for Storr. When Storr responded in kind and at length, I was genuinely shocked. Why would Storr defend his qualifications to these ninnies? Why would he bother to rebut such flimsy accusations? Then I suddenly realized, Storr is *part* of this cult! I felt as if I had just discovered that an old friend of mine belonged to Opus Dei, which is not something you judge, just something you keep in mind. So I was not surprised when Enwezor, Morgan, and Bonami shouldered their way back into the spotlight to respond at length to Storr's response. I didn't even blink when Storr re-responded to their responses to his response to their reviews of his exhibition. I was appalled by the savage manners, and saddened by the inference that power is acquired and exercised this way in the art world, but mostly I felt like a poor idiot for daydreaming about the *acqua alta* and videos of bikini girls, surfboards, and chain saws.

As an idiot, of course, I had no dog in this clash of the runt puppies, nor any feeling invested beyond my presently defunct friendship with Robert Storr. Even so, I hated the whole affair for the same reason I hate the Final Four in college basketball: it means so much to the competitors and nothing much at all to anyone else. It was a battle in a teacup, like a subteen beauty pageant. The civility of adult competition was the first casualty of this grandiosity. All sense of proportion was next, since biennial curating is no big deal. It's a support system in the service of the rich who like to see contemporary art by the bushel. This is not a big deal either. Contemporary art is a goody bag of what was fashionable last night—scraps of local "cultural production" auditioning to become art history. You can argue *for* it if you wish, but you can't argue *from* it, because not much contemporary art is very good.

To curate a persuasive international exhibition with maximum fairness and minimal redundancy, you can select maybe a hundred artists that don't overlap too terribly. Sixty of these artists would be everyone's choice. The rest would be on a majority of lists. There are no geniuses cloistered at Idaho State or in the Ukraine so, as a consequence, no matter how you divvy up the space, there will be windblown tracts of nothingness to be filled [after serial adjudications] with giant sculptures by French people, space-eating installations with TV monitors, and bad art from cultures that are famous for their bad art. Everything is too big to mean so little, which more or less guarantees a sorry exhibition.

According to Enwezor, Bonami, Morgan, and Storr, this is the big time. As if the art world were big enough for a "big time." As if being a biennial curator was a big-time gig. The guys who stock the shelves at supermarkets have more imagination, and all they do is put the sweet stuff on the bottom shelf. In my own experience, biennial curating is a blizzard of details, a river of decisions, and an ongoing effort to permit anything and touch everything. The optimal positive outcome is an exhibition that has its own music. The optimal reward is a good fee and a few quiet hours bereft of hubris in the bamboo forest with some real intellectuals.

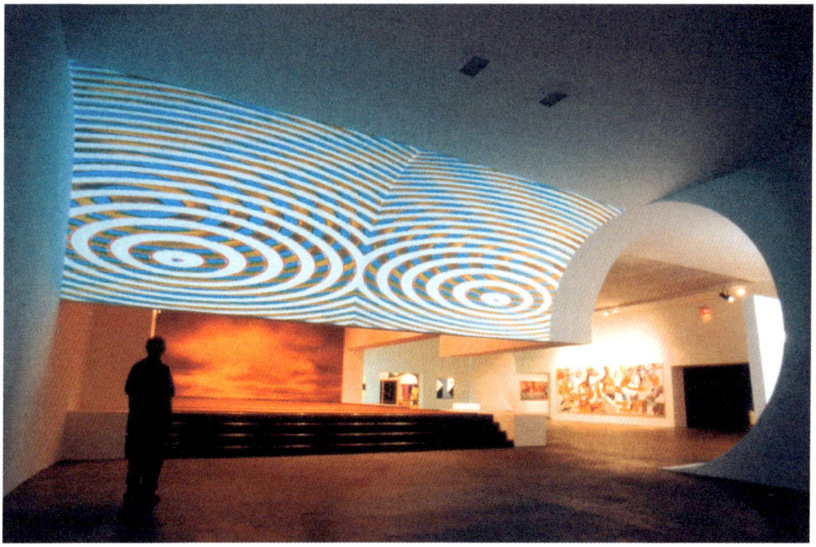

Installation view with works by Jennifer Steinkamp, Alexis Smith, Jessica Stockholder, Frederick Hammersley, James Lee Byars, Gajin Fujita, Pia Fries, and Bridget Riley. SITE Santa Fe's Fourth International Biennial, 2001, *Beau Monde: Toward a Redeemed Cosmopolitanism*, curated by Dave Hickey.

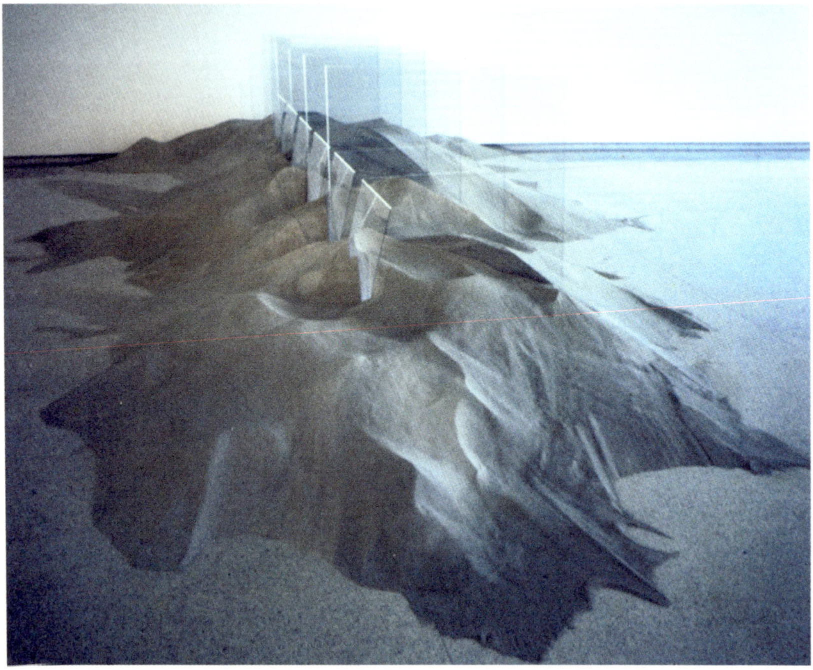

Laddie John Dill
Untitled, 1969
Sand, plate glass, argon tubing
Approx. 152 × 1066 × 244 cm | 60 × 420 × 96 in
Installation view, Walker Art Center, Minneapolis

Coping with Paradise

There is that whole shallow, indulgent, Republic-of-Trivia aspect to [Southern California] which reminds us here in New York that not since the invention of bronze casting has anything of consequence happened in that climate ... Also, the prospect of hip young dropout types hanging out in Venice, California, making fancy baubles for the rich, amuses us.

JOSEPH MASHECK, *Artforum*, 1971

THE plight of artists in the American republic has never been easy. It is no easier today. We talk a better game, but our institutional aesthetics still owe as much to John Calvin as they do to Raphael. Our public exhibition spaces still eschew Mediterranean glamour to emulate the blazing white boxes of Congregationalist chapels and Bauhaus refectories. Our Methodists and Marxists still agree on the primacy of the Word over the Flesh and the evanescence of earthly desire. So, if you're easygoing, devoid of grudges, and happen to have been popular in high school, you're in trouble. The artists from Los Angeles whose works concern me now are generally my contemporaries. They lack angst and alienation. They have grown up and spent their working lives on the continental antipode of the puritan republic—in the tropical sunshine of Southern California. So how does an artist cope with paradise when the prevailing cultural assumption is that we live in an abject world where artists are either puritan-intellectual fixer-uppers or slavish decorators?

How does an artist function in a paradise that steals the *promise* of paradise? These artists have discovered a way. Very few others, before or since, have had the modesty and equanimity to achieve this act of accommodation. Puritan intellectuals, plopped down in the perfect garden, ignore it. Slavish decorators leave no lily ungilded. Both trivialize the mysteries of the sensible world. They presume that when one fails in paradise, paradise is the problem, and it is. Traditional America is a bad-weather culture, dedicated to that brighter-day tomorrow. American Protestantism, above all else, is a bad-weather religion, directing our souls to a better "world elsewhere."

Our souls in the here and now, amid this vale of tears, are presumed to be as uncomfortable in our bodies as our bodies are in a blizzard. Perfect weather and visual equanimity steal the substance of this metaphor. They deny us visible correlatives for our historical and spiritual discomfort. They mandate a brand of art that cannot be seen or felt, that, in truth, cannot be made, only taught. Neither abject strategy or the Wizard of Oz option addresses the social consequences of living in a tropically enhanced mercantile democracy hedged in by the desert on one side and by a gargantuan body of salt water on the other. The ocean and the desert are always there: their atmospheres assure us that we live in the shimmering midst of a "full world."

The easy Euclidean distinctions that constitute the very stuff of American artistic identity dissolve. Life blurs between our bodies and our minds, our bodies and the world, between sight and touch, earth and sky, land and sea, large and small, near and far. Existing on a daily basis in a comfortable, breezy relationship with the natural climate and feeling oneself "at one" with the world, the traditional Northern European distinction between the spaces that we call negative and those we call positive evaporates—this occludes the glamour of that "world elsewhere"; it dims the past and dissolves the future in the bright mystery of the here and now.

This paradise steals our puritan souls, our hope, and our history. It leaves us in flux with no clear position from which to see, or work, or even think. We are cast adrift in a symphony of nuance, shifting emphasis, and ranging focus, and there are two straws at which to grasp: we can save our souls by ruining the garden, denying the full world, and reinstating our puritan dichotomies. *Or we can be changed by that world, make it mobile, and hope that others are changed, as well.* We can give up our puritan autonomy and gain the full world by riding the translucent waves of its sensual logic, by allowing ourselves to blur out at the edges like palm fronds in the morning fog, by devoting our most profound attention to the soft, glistening metamorphic edge of things, where straight lines curve, solids turn liquid, and liquids dissolve into atmosphere, where we can always feel the air as it moves around us off the ocean.

In this full world, there is no nothing. Nor is there any hope, history, or pretense to autonomy. Modesty, courage, and industry must suffice, and if we were to look for "internal, ongoing logic" in the work of these artists, we would find instead a flowing stream of passions and proclivities—a fluid microchronicle of the artist-as-citizen, coping with paradise with a sequence of tactile, visual solutions to specific visible occasions at the blurred interface of the artist and the world. This is what artists do in paradise: they reincarnate its domain; they make it manifest, perpetual, and mobile in its intrinsic fluidity; they try to tease its unity and complexity into some kind of eloquent, social equivalent.

The works of these artists were my first toys as a young critic, and they remain talismans of the mystery for me. In the shorthand of the art world, their work is usually referred to as Light and Space art, Fetish Finish art, or, more generally, California Minimalism. The terms don't mean much now and didn't then, but the work is still fresh. Coming upon an aggregation of these works, as I recently did, cloistered in their enduring fragility amid the chilly, industrial juggernauts of Manhattan, they feel more alien than ancient. They still bear the aura of their mysterious intentions, but they have changed. Works once decried as scandalously decorative now seem as suave as an auctioneer's couture. Objects once dismissed as the products of provincial mindlessness now manifest evidence of the most delicate ratiocination. Most interestingly, the filigree of regional, cultural, and art historical circumstance that informed the creation of these artworks is gone, and their causes and consequences are more visible now.

The overwhelming, vivifying circumstance upon which this work was founded is that the status of light and space in the American Southwest is a benign presence rather than a stark absence. This is not a world-shaking phenomenon, I know, but if you have been raised in the West, you miss it when it's gone. You miss that sense of the earth as the bottom of the sky. You miss that sense of standing *in* the world, not *on* it, more embraced than assaulted. In the northeastern United States, light from the sky is absorbed by the arboreal landscape, creating the illusion of volume and vacuum. In the Southwest, particulate dust and mist pervades the air, the light bounces back up, illuminating the atmosphere from above and below, so it presents itself to our eyes as a palpable presence. In the West, as James Turrell so aptly demonstrates, light is a thing, a local truth, and not some heavenly benison or Caravaggesque assault.

In a world without emptiness, everything that divides anything from anything else exists on the verge of dissolution or liquefaction. All surfaces seduce themselves. Even the most modest adobe wall bears the mark of its liquid youth and its particulate demise. In this work, there is hardly a surface that delivers itself to us as the exterior of the object it encloses, except for Larry Bell's boxed vacuums that bear with them the inference that hard-core "nothingness" is only visible when it is exotically and technologically isolated. All these surfaces, however, even Bell's, deliver back to us the space in which we stand, enhanced with yet more light and more space, deployed along a blended atmospheric spectrum. Laddie John Dill's works are composed of argon tubes, covered with Saharan pours of beach sand supporting vertical, intervening sheets of plate glass whose edges shine with the argon beneath the sand. Dill's pieces simultaneously manifest the multiform properties of silica and its soft spectrum of visibility: from opaque glow to atmospheric luminosity, to translucency, transparency, and reflectivity.

Dill's pieces provide an apt demonstration of what one might call an old-school Los Angeles state of mind—an attitude that derives from the city's status as what economists call a gap city, one whose culture and industry flourishes in zones that predate and postdate industrial modernity, never quite a space port, never quite a hacienda. The city runs on the manufacture of streamlined weapons, transparent narratives, fashionable clothing, decorative gardening, and sculptural architecture. As a consequence, like the California culture that nurtured it, West Coast Minimalism is intrinsically concerned with chemistry, with the slippery, unstable vernacular of oxygen, neon, argon, resin, lacquer, acrylic, fiberglass, glass, graphite, chrome, sand, and water. It floats, flashes, coats, and teases.

If East Coast Minimalism speaks the language of construction, West Coast Minimalism is more like cooking—and gourmet cooking at that. The artists who make this work, like great chefs everywhere, are necessarily concerned with appetizing presentation. These days one might be served something that looks like a Laddie Dill dune or a Craig Kauffman bubble at Lutece in Las Vegas, presented under a glass vitrine on a china plate. But presentation is just a grace note, an invitation. The *recipe* is everything. The external surfaces, which are usually dissolving before our eyes, are of no more consequence than cake pans or aspic molds. Form is not an issue; the visual conflagration of solids, liquids, and gases morphing into one another, most certainly is.

The best argument for the irrelevance of "form" in this art derives from the casual availability of the "found phenomena" these artists accumulate and exploit. New York artists gather fugitive images and structures. London artists accumulate interesting trash and antique flourishes. In my experience, there is very little California Minimalism whose exotic effects don't flash by your window on a long drive down Lincoln Boulevard, if one could but extract the diamonds from the *dreck*. The boxes, slabs, squares, piles, poles, lights, surfaces, and slashes of shadow are all redolent with allusion, but these only site the work. If the forms mean anything, they mean Los Angeles, just as Sol LeWitt's white skyscrapers and Richard Serra's slabs mean New York, and these associations are comparably trivial.

It is true enough that Robert Irwin's poles evoke the vertical interstices of palm trunks, and at LACMA they *are* palm trunks; Bell, Doug Wheeler, and Dill have all tried their hand at transparent shelving and enhanced chair rails; John McCracken's planks testify to a city under perpetual construction; Mary Corse appropriates the blaze of urban signage; and Wheeler does indeed translate the language of neon in the fog. Turrell [like John Singer Sargent in another Venice] appropriates the daunting shapes and shadows created by misty sunlight. DeWain Valentine, Kauffman, and Helen Pashgian all make off with the glamorous, technological attributes of contemporary aviation. Peter Alexander's tall wedges exactly approximate the ascending translucency of a rising wave as experienced by a surfer in the curl.

All this flutter, however, only means that the work has a home. If the atmospheric rhymes that pervade this work are mistaken for pictorial representations, or abstractions of pictorial representations, as they often were in the early criticism, the beholder is looking at something that cannot be seen. More to the point, unlike the bulk of East Coast Minimalism, this work is not *furniture*. Surrounded as it was by a culture inventing itself—by Eames design and Case Study houses—this work is best perceived as a flight from function. Worrying about what these works might "look like" or possibly do look like is like trying to see the ocean in a woozy Bridget Riley while overlooking the rich phenomenal garden of efflorescence that the artist has isolated and refined for us.

The art historical circumstances that informed the creation of West Coast Minimalism derive from a single fact. New York and California were *much* farther apart during this period than they are today. The inhabitants of these metropolises were virtually ignorant of one another. The gradual collapse of this division [caused by this art] had interesting consequences. Before this moment, art culture in America was New York bars and guys in paint-spattered pants. When Los Angeles arose as a locus of comparison, the differences were exacerbated. So the New York art world in the 1970s would claim to be as tough and puritanical as the West Coast was presumed slick and hedonistic—until the artists of New York and Los Angeles began stealing from one another—and that was that.

Early on, influence was communicated between the coasts as if by smoke signal. Works of art moved between the coasts at much greater danger and expense. The less "stuff" you shipped the better, and "nothing" shipped was better than anything. [Robert Irwin's scrims were easily shipped or purchased on site]. Also, from a mercantile perspective, this work was coming into being in the twilight of the greatest painting market for the largest paintings since the sixteenth century. All the walls were full, and conventional wisdom in both Venice and SoHo held that "the floor is the new wall"—with its California corollary that "space is the new plane." So light and space in the West were regarded as practical, proprietary, mercantile, and aesthetic virtues.

The simplest way to situate this art culturally, then, is to take an option that is rarely exploited and look at East Coast Minimalism from the West. If we do, it is immediately obvious that East Coast Minimalism is not an historical art. It is neither coming nor going. It exists in stasis as an imperial practice—the embodiment of *Pax Americana*. Donald Judd and Dan Flavin and LeWitt drew from a quiver of preconceived maneuvers and applied them to the sites and occasions that presented themselves, so the Augustan autonomy of this art was set in stone. To progress was to transgress. West Coast Minimalism, by comparison, has a softer, more indistinct lava flow; it arises from the atmospherics of midcentury modernism in Southern California, from the footprint of the freeways, the streamlined products of George Barris and Harley Earl, from the insouciance of Charles and Ray Eames, Rudolph Schindler, and Richard Neutra, and the serpentine guile of Miles Davis, John Coltrane, and Chet Baker. The hard-edge project of West Coast painters like John McLaughlin and Frederick Hammersley, who made cool look hot, was given a technological flip to make hot look cool, like the music of Art Pepper or Bud Shank.

There were no rules, in other words, and things seemed to transpire quite naturally, almost invisibly. The ambience of this scene was so thick, eccentric, and pervasive that the artists who worked in it and out of it could hardly begin to glimpse its cultural implications. As one of them told me, "All we knew was that it felt new. It felt clear, and it made you feel incredibly arrogant just being in on it." Similarly, in the late 60s, at the far end of

California Minimalism's halcyon moment, the practice dissolves quite naturally into the dishabille of Robert Smithson, Serra, Eva Hesse, Bruce Nauman, and Keith Sonnier. The rise of these artists is usually regarded as the great flowering of postindustrial art, so I should point out here, that in Postminimalism's founding moment, Nauman was working in the midst of post-industrial culture in Pasadena. Serra had just moved from Santa Barbara; the work of Dill and Smithson, McCracken, and Serra differ only in the eccentricities of local taste and the precedence of its West Coast versions. So the rise of postmodernism, or Postminimalism, or postindustrialism, or whatever it was that was posted, seems less catastrophic when viewed from the West than it does when abutted with the work of an ideological striver like Robert Morris. The change seems more like an anxious swerve of the paradigm through which the object dissolves into a physical kinaesthetic experience without being degraded in its objecthood.

Looking from the West, then, East Coast Minimalism presents itself as a handsome terminal eulogy for the romance of industrial modernism. Its underlying assumption is that if you strip the skin from any structure, you reveal another, more primary structure beneath. In the West, if you strip the skin off any structure, you reveal another skin, and another below that. So imagine this art compared to the city of Los Angeles as it presented itself to Raymond Chandler, who aspired to capture its essence. To Chandler, the Englishman, the city was an infestation, collections of detritus, tidal pools of human and cultural oddments accumulated according to no more rational principle than the tides and the prevailing winds.

So how does one address this human cauldron? Traditional aesthetics routinely demand some meaningful relationship between form and content, but liquids, however heterogeneous, take the form of their enclosure. So Chandler took the next best option for his subject. *À ficelé* connectedness of formlessness—

this is Chandler's content. He invented the LA private-eye narrative as a crooked spit around which the cultural enclaves of Los Angeles might seem to revolve—a loosely woven web of occasions and confrontations, revelations and unfoldings, that runs like a biodegradable armature through the tidal pool. The subject of Chandler's books is fully functioning entropy, the exoticism and banality of the chaos through which Philip Marlowe slides on his quests. The actual narrative of what happens and what happens next is no more relevant than the plot of *Don Quixote*, or *Tristram Shandy*, or Bell's cubes, or Kauffman's bubbles, or McCracken's planks. They tell the story, but the story is a totally artificial container for the kinesthetic atmospherics that constitute the actual subject matter of the work.

Unsurprisingly, the unavoidable abyss between form and content in California Minimalism and in Chandler's books left both of them open to criticism from critics who find the artificial plot, as necessary as it is, a terminal fault. All this really means is that in the kingdom of liquid entropy you bring your own bucket, and you want the most elegant bucket you can imagine because, even though the object was largely discredited at that critical moment, there is no persuasive reason that objects existing as kinesthetic sites should be ugly or insist on their obsolescence. In the war against form, one begins to wonder just how often a point need be made to be discredited.

So, finally, having alluded to this work in terms of couture and cuisine, I should speak about its elegance, because this is elegant work, pleasing, ingenious, economical, and neat; this attribute was as astonishing in its moment as it seems today. In its initial vogue, these works of art spoke directly to a new kind of artistic decorum—less aggressive than Pop, less disheveled than Abstract Expressionism, less ideological than Minimalism, and less maidenly than Post-Painterly Abstraction. It had a kind of gallantry—the cool courtesy of a well-born rake. In a moment when Clement Greenberg was advocating febrile sensibility and Michael Fried was demanding that works of art ignore our presence like unloving fathers, California Minimalism created a gracious social space in its glow and reflection; it treated us amicably and made us more beautiful by gathering us into the dance. It still does this today, so I am not amazed by the renewed interest. I am still amazed that my beach-bum pals could have created such a capacious and courtly art. Beach bums, I suppose, have dreams like everyone else.

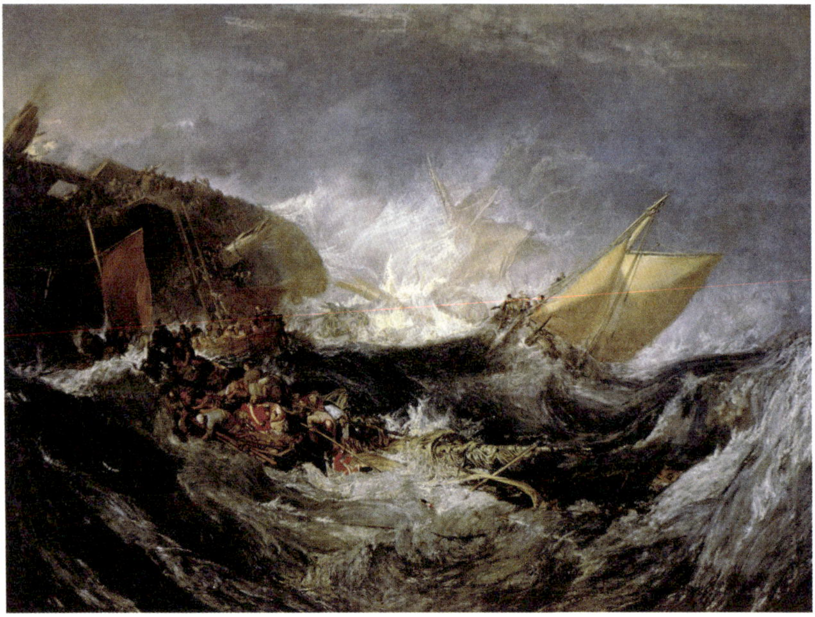

Joseph Mallord William Turner
Wreck of a Transport Ship, c.1810
Oil on canvas
172.7 × 241.2 cm | 68 × 95 in

Orphans in the Storm

In 1961, when Edward Ruscha returned to Los Angeles from an art-intense trip to Italy, someone asked him what he found. Edward shrugged and said: "Oh, lots of things, but nothing I could use." Last week, I heard this remark cited as evidence that young artists might safely ignore the art of the past. This is not quite what Edward said. He said he was *looking* for something that he could use and didn't find anything on this visit to Italy. Over the length of his career, however, Ruscha has found so *much* in the past to use that ignoring his artistic precedents diminishes our experience of his paintings. Regarding Italy, it would better to note that, having been raised a Roman Catholic, Ruscha had already received his great Italian bequest in the mystery of the Eucharist [*Wonder Bread*, 1962], in the *Standard Stations* of the Cross [1966], and the doctrine of the Incarnate Word that is made modern and manifest in Ruscha's work.

These appropriations constitute a considerable debt to the past—and to Italy—but they are far from the only ones. As a landscape painter, Ruscha virtually loots the nineteenth century, which, when Edward was a young artist, was an unfashionable suburb ripe for the looting. He appropriated Frederic Church's glamorous horizon-line atmospheres. He transformed Caspar David Friedrich's ghostly square riggers into meditations on motion and memory. He set his incarnate words afloat in concave spaces borrowed from John Everett Millais's *Ophelia* [1851–52], a copy of which he keeps pinned to his studio wall. At the 51st Venice Biennale in 2005, Ruscha represented the US with a suite of paintings that update Thomas Cole's series of paintings *The Course of Empire* [1833–36]. The idea of sending new American paintings to Venice, based on old American paintings that flaunt their own debt to Venetian painting, is just the sort of ring-around-the-rosy that appeals to Ruscha.

If you look at artworks as I do, against a field of all the artworks you've ever seen, this intricate flutter of precedents makes for a bigger and more memorable experience, and size matters in one's experience of art. Lately, I've been missing that resonant thickness in the art I see in galleries. Contemporary art, having lost its utopian future, now seems to be losing its usable past. The fashionable opacity of too much new art seems comfortably ensconced at the level of enigmatic decor, like Olafur Eliasson's work, which is a bit like Siegfried without Roy—although it would be enhanced by white tigers. The ruthless difficulty to which artists once aspired is now held in abeyance because they dare not be snobs anymore. The art world has lowered its entrance requirements so precipitously and raised its cover charge so radically that a couple of million bucks, a casual acquaintance with Hilary Swank, and a passing familiarity with comic books, will gain one entrée into the most refined salon. As a result, the contemporary artist's field of play, once defined by the collective knowledge and experience of artists and cognoscenti, has gone to seed. The groundskeepers have all gone home.

To keep money on the table, the core agenda of Pop art has been reversed. Pop artists snapped up the sprawling ephemera of popular culture, invested it with beaux arts rigor, and gave it a shot at immortality. "Reverse Pop" artists make their new audience comfortable by investing tropes of beaux arts integrity with the biodegradable flimsiness of popular culture. Andy Warhol made art masquerading as pop. Richard Prince makes pop masquerading as art. John Currin, having outgrown his subject, forges adolescent nymphs. Jeff Koons seems capable of walking the edge of this shiny razor with gargantuan "goody-bag" trophies, but, even so, the idea of dispensing with the touchable residue of a 500-year cultural inheritance remains very mysterious to me.

I meet artists every day who are only thirty years further removed from the historical past than Ruscha and I. They seem centuries more remote from that past, and not because we are old and they are young. Ruscha and I and most of our peers found the past when *we* were their age because *we* were looking for a way *out*—not a way *in*. We were looking for precedents upon which to found a revolution—submerging ourselves in the murky swamp of unfashionable objects, stretching our toes downward to find a new bottom from which we might push off. We wanted things that we could use, things we could steal, borrow, misappropriate, or crosspollinate.

Given this background, I should probably complain that young artists no longer seek out revolutionary precedents. I can't, because, in a practical sense, those precedents are not there anymore. The usable past has been sent home without its supper. Postcolonialists, identity politicians, and visual theorists, and New York anticosmopolitans have returned all hard precedents to their original owners. These originating cultures, classes, races, places, and genders now have all their toys back to do with as they will—and the Afghans sure fixed those Buddhas up nice. This leaves the rest of us, like the children in *Bleak House*, perpetually in Chancery, unable to claim our rightful cultural inheritance.

So we are bereft. Three decades of art theory and the Brownian motion of cryptoaesthetic mayflies has destroyed our memory of art as a stochastic practice of sentient mammals in the physical world where nothing is exempted and nothing is obsolete. The practices of law, medicine, and art are dedicated to maintaining and renewing our ideas of justice, safety, and happiness. Each hold a full field of nonprioritized precedents, ready to cope with the unprecedented present. Everything is always available because you never know what antique legal decision, herb, or image you will need right now at the event horizon.

So art, as chic theory, may be disembodied ideas. Art, as narrative history, may be remote from the present and a lie. Artworks themselves, however, are orphans in the storm, permanent practical precedents, forever young, forever free, and physically here with us. Theoretical constructs may hold their place in a field of knowledge. Historical artifacts may speak of their ancestry and parental origins. Works of art, as orphans in the storm, are ready to be adopted, nurtured, and groomed to the needs of any astonishing new circumstance.

New law and new medicine arise from a shifting field of precedents as a hedge against injustice and disease. New art arises from a shifting field of precedents as a hedge against ennui, and these precedents never die. Their apparent precedence is *caused* by the present, and this precedence should be ignored. The old past goes in and a new future comes out. The kernel of influence, like Alice, slips through the looking glass. Local contexts and intentions are moot compared to the consequences of the Magna Carta, the birth of contract law, and the Declaration of Independence; the discovery of penicillin, anesthesia, and mapping the genome; compared to the making of the *Mona Lisa*, *Las Meninas,* and *Blue Poles*.

The future arises out of misprision, misinterpretation, contemporary needs, and pure contingency. Or it would, were it not for the long decades of swampy ground once populated by merry bands of performers, installers, scatterers, mimes, jugglers, and exhibitionists that lie between ourselves and the world of invention and objects. This marsh was once a bourgeois carnival. Today, the pranks are well documented; some by me [masquerading, unwillingly, as a drama critic], but this past is not there anymore. Today, it is documents and archives—catnip for scholars, historians, critics, and artists who prefer to reimagine Shakespeare by reading the reviews. In the world of theory, seeking anything useful of the sort Ruscha sought in Italy is like playing poker with no spots on the cards.

Although I was educated as a linguistic theorist, I like being an art critic better, because anyone who disagrees with me can go look at the thing itself and decide for him or herself about the justice of my argument. On the topic of ephemeral art, however, I am *the man* for my students. I have seen it from the inside, as Jonah saw the whale. I am Marco Polo back from China, Jesus back from the tomb. With no extant restraints like real objects in the world, I can say whatever pops into my mind, and it is probably wrong. Many of my colleagues enjoy this clerical privilege more than I and more than they should. They seek to influence young artists, and they do. They have also destroyed the engine of change—the "anxiety of influence" [as Harold Bloom called it] that arises when artists come to terms with art that will not go away, that holds its place in the world. So, if you choose to flaunt fashion and be influenced by, say, Pablo Picasso, you had better do something cool with Picasso to justify doing anything at all.

This does not mean that Picasso *owns* Picasso. It means that Picasso painted many great Picassos, so any new work in the manner of Picasso requires some fillip of innovation as a *raison d'être*. You can't just preempt The Pablo. He's there, and you must swerve or squeeze around him. In this way, the persistence of the past encourages refinement and style change. In the great age of ephemeral art, however, style change was presumed defunct because history was presumed dead. The latter was true. The narrative of history almost certainly died during this period.

But *time did not stop*, nor has any object of art that existed in or before that moment ceased to exist. Art is not science or technology. Extant works of art are never obsolete. They succumb to the whims of fashion and move to the unfashionable suburbs, where Ruscha found Cole, where they remain at the ready, until what is cool at the moment begins to bore us.

Tedium swings the pendulum in the practice of art, so art history is more geological than teleological, less a story than a sequence of abrupt earthquakes and cataclysms, each of which changes everything. The pressure builds up and boom! Raphael, Caravaggio, Manet, Picasso, Pollock, Warhol, and Koons. They got it right the first time, so we spend our time between quakes adapting to the last quake, never imagining there will be another until we start getting bored. Then, when we feel the change coming, all we know is that the "fashionable" will not be replaced by the "postfashionable." It will be obliterated by the "unfashionable," scrounged in some dingy suburb and brought forth, fresh as a baby, by some dumpster-diving young troublemaker. With every quake, the tectonic hierarchy of past precedents is reordered, but nothing goes away.

Ephemeral art does go away. It holds its place in books, pictures, and folklore, but not in the world, so artists influenced by ephemeral art needn't be anxious about influence. If you want to do Bruce Nauman or Jason Rhoades, go to it. The short attention span of your audience will quickly make it yours. Or, you could emulate the duke and the dauphin in *Huckleberry Finn* and take it to Arkansas or Java where nobody's seen anything. There are two lawsuits on my desk right now from whistleblowers seeking my counsel on government grants inadvertently given to artists in Latin America who do the work of young Asian artists. It's all just there out in the drift. When I played in a band, there was always some idiot in the audience who thought we wrote "Tumbling Dice"—or that he did. Once, in a true Rachel

Whiteread moment, while trying to write a song, I inadvertently wrote new lyrics to the melody of Tom Waits's "Ol' 55." In the big, poopy pile of popular culture, this is stupid but explicable. In the global art world, these "appropriations" seem sort of cheesy and gross, but by the time we decide that the sliced-up shark is mundane, it will be too big to fail.

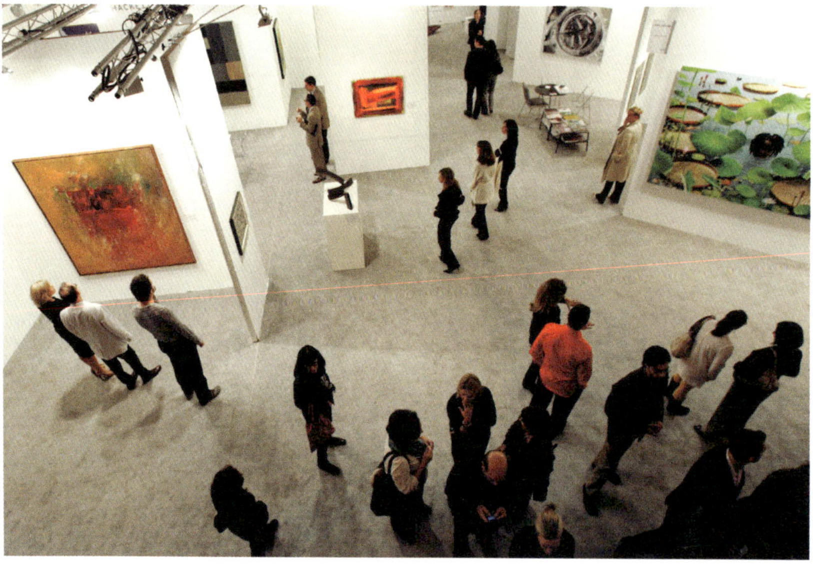

Art Miami private view, 2008

Vogue

I BECAME an art critic because I wanted to tell the truth, and works of art seemed small enough and impersonal enough to tell the truth about without making much of a fuss. I had one ambition: I wanted to write well enough that my writing would be there for the reckoning, so I thought of myself as a gardener, like my grandmother. I wanted to pull up the weeds and water the roses. Now that the weeds are more expensive than the roses, this is impossible, and my preferences, I'll admit, may be completely wrong. The future may go where it seems to be going, but I am still interested in vogue, in the tides of public taste. In a book called *Private Truths, Public Lies: The Social Consequences of Preference Falsification* [1995], Timur Kuran shares this interest.

Kuran's book is about economics and politics, but his statistical insights apply to anything about which our public preferences are solicited, voted, volunteered, up for sale, or demanded. Kuran argues with good statistics that a healthy percentage of all publicly articulated preferences are falsified because of individual perversity, the temper of the government, or the pressure of majority opinion. The percentage of truthfully stated preferences in any survey usually varies from forty to sixty percent of the total preferences solicited or volunteered. The percentage of falsified preferences, however, goes up as truthful preferences move into the majority. So, if fifty-five percent of respondents honestly prefer the work of, say, Gary Hume, seventy-five percent will say they do. Twenty-five percent will be lying, for whatever reason.

Kuran and I are interested in the dynamics of publicly stated preferences and the catastrophic reversals they undergo. Kuran wants to know how a Czechoslovak might go to bed a professed communist in Prague in December of 1989 and wake up the next morning as a fierce democrat. I am interested in how an art critic in New York might go to bed a devoted Situationist and wake up a devotee of neo-Mogul painting. In Kuran's research, once the *stated preferences* achieve a majority, they exhibit enormous inertia, but there is an inverse variable at work. As the percentage of stated preferences increases, the *actual* number of *honest* preferences erodes. The percentage of lies escalates toward a tipping point where the most fleeting occasion can swing the scale. In a volatile market, this means that our preferences for artworks are most vulnerable when they reach their cynosure. I call it the "been there, done that" factor, and the visible causes of these public mood swings can seem so trivial that it looks like a mouse ate the moon.

Even so, why would a dishonest election in Iran (which has never had an honest election) send people into the streets? Twitter? Why would someone pay a sum of money, roughly equivalent to our total aid to Palestine, for a work by Jeff Koons and put it in a warehouse? I respect Jeff's work, but not as much as the population of Palestine. The only answer I can imagine is that people have been lying about Koons and Palestine for a long time, and I don't excuse myself. Like Niccolò Machiavelli, I became so interested in the whir of the big machine early on that I got my sleeve caught up in the gears. Now I am in exile. All my patrons and mentors are dead. Now, I lie too, by commission or omission, out of courtesy or kindness to hosts, artists, and collectors. Like Ovid, I fritter my days away in a provincial resort writing up my dreams.

In my dream last night, I was strolling past an art fair booth. An art consultant in pale couture was cuddling up to a Joe-Pesci-type guy in a flashy Zegna suit. They were looking at a hideous, red-and-blue gouache, framed, matted, and set up on a white stand. Awkward daubs of gouache extended out onto the framing mat—as if that were a cool thing to do. [Things like this happen in dreams.] In this dream, I knew these people and bade them good day. Joe Pesci grabbed my arm and pulled me in.

"Hey, Dave," he said, "What do you think about this Picasso? How much? Give me a guesstimate."

The gouache was not a Picasso. It was hardly even art, but I didn't want to be rude to either party. I pretended to ponder. Joe reached up, grabbed my shoulder in a vice-like pinch that made my knees buckle, and repeated his question more firmly.

"What do you think about this Picasso?" he demanded.

Then I woke up, feeling yucky, as usual, because this is not an unusual type of dream for me. Nor is it an unusual type of experience in my waking life. The art world is a very vulgar place if you are not pathologically servile. Over the years, it has bestowed dreams in a variety of formats on me. In most of these dreams, I am being shown through a dim, Brooklyn loft complex full of laptops, sleeping bags, industrial music, and huge, crummy, adolescent billboards that I am expected to validate. I have never made it all the way through this studio visit in dreamland. Usually, right before I wake up, I'm thinking about trading a touch of faint praise for some drugs to get me back to the land of tall buildings.

I'm not really complaining, though. Looking at art in the presence of its owners or creators is part of my job. I make it harder for myself by expecting something magical and trying to be candid without being cruel. To avoid crushing hopes, I withhold disapprobation. I say, "This is autobiographical, right?" Or, "Hey, this is really something!" Or, as Gary Indiana once concluded in a review of Sherrie Levine's work: "If you've never seen plywood, you're in for a treat." Even this is dangerous. On my last visit to the graduate studios at Yale, I discovered the institution founded by my ancestors going through a rough patch of wolverine ambition, so have I stopped going to New Haven.

In any case, unless I'm on the clock or under contract, I still play it straight. I don't do numbers. When pressed too fiercely about the value of a putative Picasso, I suggest the patient consult Acquavella or Pace, presuming that Bill and Arne will be less accessible than I am. Actually, even if the painting in my dream *had been* a Picasso, I wouldn't have said that it was. I am not a public utility. The advantage of my knowing and their not knowing is just too enormous—the time invested in learning how to recognize a Picasso [or a *really* good fake] is too valuable to give away. In this case, I would have called Acquavella or Pace and done them what might turn out to be a favor.

I thought these thoughts this morning sitting on the edge of my bed, realizing, even as I thought them, how pretentious they seemed. I was behaving as if the things I said and wrote had something to do with art history, and I still wish they did. Today, I only participate in the murmuring, ongoing cascade of hints, nods, critiques, scholarly speculations, and acquisitions that buoy up works of art in public vogue, that bear them forward from the moment of their creation to the wall in front of us, where they hang as fresh and new as the day they were created.

So if you are feeling a bit down about the state of your career, check out some *Artforum* magazines from the 1980s and 90s and peruse all the art that hasn't survived. This art didn't just evanesce or die of natural causes. Art doesn't get colic like my sister's horses or contract pulmonic stenosis like the first of my three beagles named Ralph. Art has to be killed. Sometimes this happens accidentally—by war, fire, or flood, the Taliban, or Ralph the Beagle, who ate a very nice Alex Katz lithograph that I carelessly left on the dining-room table. Usually, art is murdered. Sometimes this is a good idea. Someone kills it, crushes it, blows it up, abandons it in storage, or recycles it, and the world has lost or won.

Today, since negative reviews don't exist anymore, there is a job I would really like to have: Official Art Executioner of the United States and Europe. I have been practicing for this position my whole life, and I would like to be officially recognized as such. I am not a power freak; nor do I desire a TV show. I am kind, patient, methodical, and tolerant of promising talent. As saintly as I am, however, if we're just talking about art, I could still empty three-quarters of the lofts in Brooklyn, because I do not care about the artistic careers of losers who would be better off throwing pizza dough. I am not suggesting that all of this art be destroyed, however, some of it should be just thrown away. Art, like culture, should be allowed to grow. There is a saying in the barrios of South Central Los Angeles that it takes two generations to get out of the hood. Some art takes two artists to finish the work, like Picasso's contemptuous redo of Jean Cocteau's portrait of Dora Maar.

The best art-rescue project I know took place in the early 70s in SoHo. Everybody was painting those 8 × 12-foot abstract squeegee paintings. You could only reprime these canvases so many times, so a lot of canvas [prewaterproofed] got thrown out. Homeless dudes started collecting it. Soon, a vacant lot on Prince near Broadway was hosting the most elegant Bedouin encampment in the world. We called it Lyrical Abstractionville, and trust me: a bad painting can make a lovely tent in a field of lovely tents. Today it would get a foundation grant after being ransacked by the police. At the time, the tents were just ransacked by the police.

Usually, fate is not so kind. In the 80s, when money was just getting slippery, an "art professional" I know quietly deaccessioned some surplus Neoexpressionism to a Colombian drug lord for some clandestine cash. The drug lord hung the paintings in his house, which, not long thereafter, was leveled by an explosion of unknown origin. My point: at every juncture in the existence of a work of art there are people whose preference is not falsified, who care or don't care, who make life or death decisions about art's survival. Some are just being bitchy and some are not. I think art history should catalogue these fluid adventures, its heroes and villains. It should begin when the work is born and trace its travels, adventures, ambushes, narrow escapes, and triumphs through the centuries or the hours.

I have always insisted that a work's physical provenance tells us things we need to know. Now, I must insist that an artwork's *intellectual provenance* would tell us nearly everything. What if we traced the fate of Kimberly's shag-rug portrait of Barack Obama, created for her graduate exhibition? What if we had a catalogue of every written, musical, and visual reference to Velázquez's *Las Meninas* [1656], from the earliest documents up to and including Eve Sussman's video *89 Seconds at Alcázar* [2004] and the Spanish girl band called Las Meninas, that I just invented in my head?

Then we would know the true fate of Kimberly's shag-rug, and we would have this gigantic, multicultural chronicle of what human beings, having seen *Las Meninas*, have written, painted, and sung over three-and-a-half centuries. And we would still have *Las Meninas*, the real physical object on hand in Madrid. Velázquez's painting, seen through the multiple lenses of protean encounters, would put us as close as we are likely to get to an empirical history of the changing social construction of our visual expectations. Multiply this chronicle by a hundred and the benefits would be extraordinary. We could see Jackson Pollock's *Autumn Rhythm* [1950] standing still as sequential interpretations sweep over it, like multihued mist. We could ponder what it means to love a disobedient object so much that we continually make up new excuses for its existence.

This is why exiled typists like myself battle the escalating tsunami of self-serving hypocrisy. Most people lie about what they like or love. I lie as well these days just to get through to the veal. If I were the Official Art Executioner, however, you would still have to invite me to dinner because you don't want to piss me off. At the same time, I would not have to proclaim my undying appreciation of Luc Tuymans just to get to the main course. I would be obligated to address dissimulation wherever I found it, and this would be *official*. There would be an oath. I could be the bad guy. Mister Clean-Out-Your-Locker and Turn-in-Your-Playbook. I could kick you out of grad school. Republicans would invite me to the Hamptons until they figured me out. Organized opposition and factions would rise up. There would be riots and demonstrations against my hegemony; "occupiers" with signs and bullhorns could gather in front of my house. A new underground would arise and grow. When it was big enough, I would quit my executioner gig and join the new underground. Then I would be back where I belong.

This would be great. I could continue to do what I do anyway. I wrote about Norman Rockwell because friends who professed to hate Rockwell, really didn't. I wrote about Robert Mapplethorpe because friends who professed to love his work, really didn't. In both cases, falsified preferences needed to be nudged toward the tipping point. Rockwell and Mapplethorpe needed new excuses to validate their own brands of naughtiness. Pollock needs a new *raison d'être* every year or so. So let me suggest that we regard works of art as species that adapt or perish, and suggest, as Luther Burbank might, that hybridization may be the answer. Finally, let me suggest that we shouldn't falsify our preferences just to get invited to dinner. It has consequences.

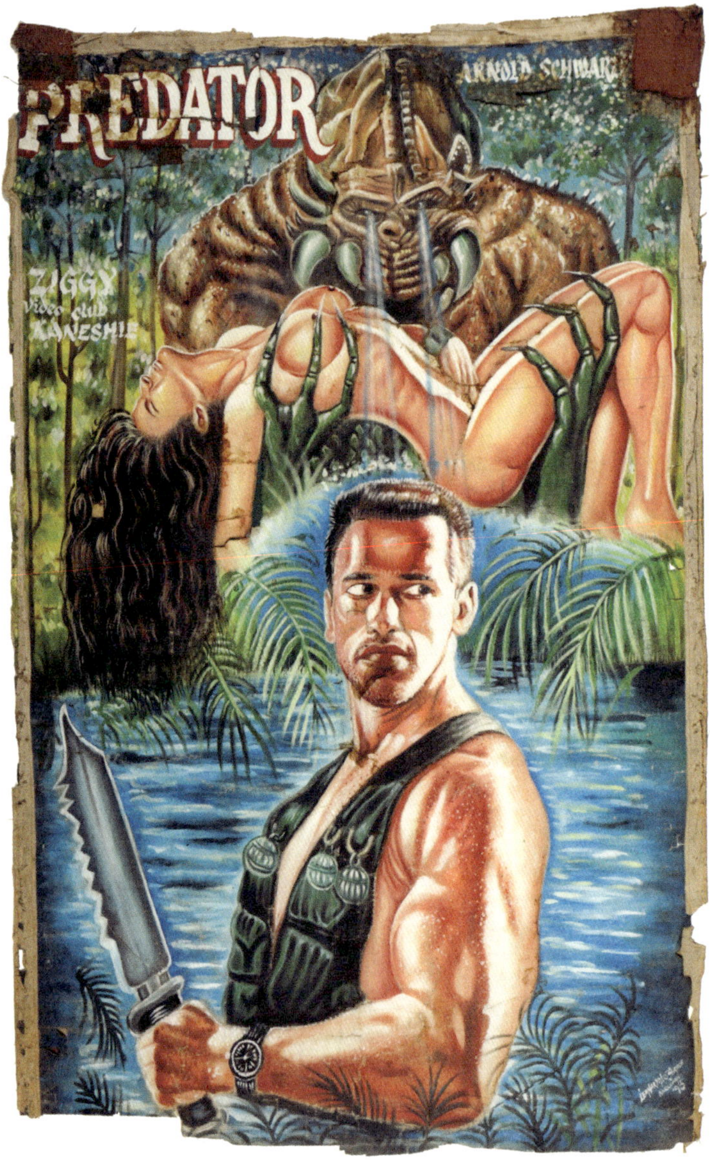

Leonardo
Predator, 1993
Oil on cotton canvas
193 × 127 cm | 76 × 50 in

In the Sunshine of Absolute Neglect

THE flowering of Ghanaian movie-poster painting filled a serendipitous technological gap in the 1980s and 90s. During this period, imported action movies were circulated in the Ghanaian bush on VCR; they were shown on old television sets powered by portable generators. Printed promotional graphics were not available, so promotional paintings were commissioned from local sign painters to advertise forthcoming showings of *The Terminator* and *Commando*. The painters took justified credit for "crowd pulling," which became a sign of status, and the paintings set them free.

The imported movies privileged the sex and violence that is frowned upon in mainstream Ghanaian culture. The artists could advertise their imagination of Hollywood hotties and the washboard abs of local gym rats, albeit with Dolph Lundgren's face. Until that moment, these painters had been relegated to painting bananas, mangos, oranges, cell phones, and barbershop portraits of Brad Pitt with the coolest, new, peroxide-shorty dreads. These new paintings were a big step up—gauche, grandiose, and confident—with mucus-dripping cobras, predatory farangs in camo, AK-47s, naked girls, aliens, severed feet, and blood-dripping scimitars. Adapting their domestic talents to these movie paintings obliterated their un-American modesty and they became real artists.

They became famous; they assembled ateliers; they carried forward a West African tradition that still persists in America's Black communities, happily investing their time and fame in the education of young artists as students, interns, and apprentices—an honorable tradition in their little window of fame. When they were the Playboys and the Bad Boys too, there was nothing like them. They painted their posters on fifty-kilogram flour-sacks split, flattened, and conjoined into vertical billboards. This flour sack design became their signature of authenticity.

During their short, bright spring, these paintings belonged to the same class of Ghanaian objects as the carved and elaborately embellished figurative coffins of fire trucks, turtles, and dragons ordered to taste and created by the carvers of Accra. The patrons intended to be buried in these FAV, or "Fantastic Afterlife Vehicles," although, as often as not, the coffins survived. Collectors snapped them up as originals to rescue their grandiosity from interment. The carver carved a duplicate, occasionally delighting the patron, occasionally selling the copy as an original. They were not savages; they were cosmopolitan people who understood buzz. They knew the difference between what we want and what we want to see. In the midst of these coffins, paintings, and Ashanti designs, one cannot help but be worldly. Everything is open to interpretation, and some are as bloody and boisterous as Titian's *The Flaying of Marsyas* (c. 1570–76).

It may seem frivolous to take such marginal productions seriously, but it's important to remember that the paintings, coffins, and Ashanti designs of Ghana are cosmopolitan objects that remain a part of quotidian Ghanaian life. They have not been "vitrinified" or sequestered. They have their daily functions. By the counterintuitive logic of popular entertainment, the violence of the action-movie paintings compensated for the quiet lives of kids in the bush who, like kids everywhere, lifted heavy things, ran around in circles, and played football because that's all there was to do.

To save them, every week or so, a couple of local entrepreneurs in ball caps, dreads, and Hawaiian shirts set off into the bush like time travelers into the past. They would chug up the river or bounce along muddy trails on a bus with a VCR, a twenty-inch television, two speakers, a generator, and a bundle of filmed adventures from Hollywood, Bollywood, Hong Kong, and local West African studios. The artists, of course, had to start painting while the dudes with the tapes were still chugging up the river or bumping down the road. They hadn't even *seen* the movie they were advertising. They had some stills or a throwaway flyer, so creative latitude was required and even encouraged. The artists had to preadapt the foreign movies to local tastes *après la lettre*. Bruce Lee and Arnold Swarzenegger took on aggressive postures and tribal scowls that would have made Picasso wee-wee in delight.

As this jungle film festival progressed, styles evolved. Fights were fought and things caught fire. Styles became more eccentric as artists maneuvered for competitive advantage. Reputations spread. The images took on a visual life distinct from the films they advertised. People collected these paintings, bought them, stole them, or threw the worst away. Gradually the paintings overpowered the movies on which they were based—as Renaissance painting overpowered their devotional narratives—because they were better. The paintings "Africanized" the iconography of the action and adventure film, and I like to think they represent the Dark Continent's droll revenge on modernism.

The European and American devotees of modernist primitivism routinely mistake the offhand friskiness of African art for solemnity. Art is not a laughing matter to devotees, so connoisseurs invariably find Picasso's painted version of a carved Yoruban breast superior to a starlet's boobies filtered through ebullient Ghanaian imaginations. Call it revenge, but it would be fairer to assume that everyone was in on the joke—that most viewers took in the snakes-guns-and-boobs idiom with a whimsical little Bill Cosby grin. These were Western guns and boobs, after all, and imaginary monsters.

When the martial arts market began to fade, like American artists after the Revolution, these painters devoted themselves to what Ernie Wolfe calls "praise paintings" of celebrities and honored leaders.[1] In Ghanaian praise portraits, Barack Obama, Bob Marley, Jerry Rawlings, Bill Clinton, and Nelson Mandela stand in for the Founding Fathers. Even so, by the time digital printing supplanted their endeavors, there was a nationwide community of artists in Ghana hard at work. The most visible of these artists, El Anatusi, broke the regional bubble by blending Ghana and the manner of the beaux arts West.

El Anatusi recreates the grandeur of Ghana's riotous fecund bush from the detritus of industrial civilization—liquor-bottle caps, lids from tins of concentrated milk, and silver vinyl wrappers. He hangs gigantic scrims, evoking the tangled grandeur of his native land, made from the dead trash of ours. He also makes piles of bent and folded junk, many of which have been most recently displayed at the Brooklyn Museum. El Anatusi, of course, has the virtue of being "in style" at the moment, making art made for export to celebrate and critique Ghana itself, but there are other exquisite objects and paintings being made in Ghana. There are paintings, mostly family portraits, executed in a highly exoticized manner reminiscent of Gérôme. You will never see them because they don't look African enough. They seem to be the product of asteroids colliding, which is not far from wrong.

None of this Ghanaian bouquet could have blossomed, however, if Ghana were not the special place that it is. If Ghana were *really* dangerous, like Somalia or the Ivory Coast, the artists would be dead and their paintings burned. Ghanaians are more relaxed—more concerned with their cell phones and iPods than the rigors of doctrine. Two of the greatest painters in this tradition, Babs and the late Muslim, were Muslims themselves. They worried less about Islamic iconophobia than developing a dry-brush painting technique that mimicked the sprayed blur of Los Angeles graffiti. This isn't to say that Ghana isn't dangerous. It's about as dangerous as Renaissance Rome—which was liveable but no stroll on *la Grande Jatte*.

This cultural climate exists because Ghana inherited a nonfactional tradition of civil administration from the ancient Ghanaian Empire. For centuries preceding colonialism, Ghana's peoples were accustomed to a government that was nontribal, nonethnic, nonreligious, nonmilitary, and tolerant of a civil service that offered career opportunities for the easily corrupted. Ghana was the first colonial protectorate to achieve independence. It was blessed from jump with serious, well-educated leaders like Kwame Nkrumah, Kofi Atta Annan, and most prominently, by Rawlings, who staged a bloody military coup, then came to his senses.

Ultimately, Rawlings would re-establish democracy in Ghana. He modernized the state, put things in order, reclaimed stolen revenues from bureaucrats' bank accounts and redistributed the money to public ends. He was no saint [and half-white to boot], but he initiated free elections that have persisted. Rawlings's greatest moment, like George Washington's, was stepping down alive. Rawlings attended the inauguration of his successor, John Kufuor, and of John Atta Mills, who died in 2012 and remains the most intellectual of Ghana's presidents. As a consequence, almost alone among African nations, Ghana has a tradition of peaceful elections and transitions of power, with only the occasional Jeffersonian coup.

This, I suspect, is why Ghanaians are more ironic, less excitable, and less exotic than most of their neighbors. English is the official language, and its patois is everywhere audible in the United States and the Caribbean. The patois traces back to the days when Accra was a major slave port—the fictional setting of Randy Newman's "Sail Away." Ghana is also blessed with rich, exportable natural resources—cocoa, gold, and oil—whose profitability encourages a civil mercantile environment. The profits from these exports, like those in our own country, trickle down slowly to the populace, but they do trickle down, so there is as much hope as despair in the countryside.

The cultural capital of Ghana resides in Kumasi in the heart of Ashanti country, a tribal nation known for its haughty arrogance, kente cloth, graphic fabrics, and passion for design. During World War II, my old friend Julian Stanczak was a Jewish kid from Russia who crawled from beneath a pile of dead bodies in the Ukraine and made his way south. He is now an Op artist of international renown who was taught to paint by the Ashanti in a refugee camp on the outskirts of Kumasi. Julian lives in Cleveland now and shows with Lucy Mitchell at Mitchell-Innes and Nash. The painter Kwame Akoto, aka Almighty God, rules Kumsai's culture with his eponymous swagger. No one in "biennial land" pays attention. They need their art presorted. They can't distinguish fine art from folk art or commercial art in a nonsegregated bouillabaisse like quotidian Ghana. They can, at least in the case of El Anatusi, recognize dominant installation art, and good for them.

My pivotal point is that artistic Ghana is far from exceptional in cosmopolitan cultures where art is chosen and not accredited or anointed. The flowering of painting, carving, and design in Ghana represents the same evolution from barbarity into civilization that always takes place when cultures are allowed to evolve from killing to fighting to playing to performing. This happens everywhere democracy is more than an idea in some professor's head, wherever the outside world is available with surprises. There is always a golden moment between the garden, the greenhouse, and the vitrine. The process is worldwide.

In America, it began in the tribal neighborhoods of New Orleans and spread to the ethnic hoods of our large cities. It begins with tribal rivalries, tiny wars over territory, drive-by shootings, fights, and insults concerning one's mother's virtue.

These confrontations evolve into competitions like boxing, football, martial arts, and basketball. The winner has the most points at the end of the game, or the winner is the survivor in competitive confrontations of rhymed insults at improv-comedy clubs or "cutting contests" at B-boy dances and jazz concerts, where improvisation follows improvisation into the night until the loser ultimately runs out of moves, notes, or rhymes, so we always know who won and the tribes stay intact.

Then there is a cosmopolitan trigger, like mass-produced Nikes in California or mass-produced musical instruments in New Orleans. Eventually, hand-eye coordination is refined. Hand-ear coordination starts hitting the note. Recordings are available. The intellectual exuberance and dazzling verbal facility of "calling the dozens" creates the Elizabethan babel of rap. These skills combined are elevated into performances. The winner becomes a "star" whose status is decided upon by shared social standards. So "taste" has evolved as a calm stratosphere for raw tribal desire. Both sides agree on the winner; the gap is bridged and civilization has arisen—or "civilization is a rose," as Gertrude Stein put it—in the same way that tagging, B-boy, and rap overpowered the street gangs that created them to claim power and territory.

It begins as a gang fight and ends as a work of art, like *Romeo and Juliet*. A new canon of taste and desire now bridges local differences. A society of peers agree on something, and we're not talking folk art here, or high art or commercial art. We're talking about people *choosing* art from the creative consequences of cosmopolitan chaos. Rivalries move from combat to consensus. In the mid-70s, the dance critic Sally Banes took me uptown on the train to see kids dancing to a boom box. They were spinning on flattened cardboard boxes on a sidewalk in a shell-shocked neighborhood in the Bronx.

They called their dance "B-boy" (or as one kid put it "hoops for short dudes"). With their top rocks, helicopters, freezes, scraps, and suicides, they created that Oh-my-God-this-is-really-new fizz in my gut. This was the last time I felt that effervescence, and I was right. Six weeks later these kids were dancing on Broadway and TV for actual money. Such elevations took place in Renaissance Rome, in bebop New York, in hip hop, and in the flowering of Ghanaian paintings and coffins. It is rough democracy, but rough is what democracy does best. Like the culture of LA graffiti, objects aren't protected. They last as long as we love them and they give us pleasure. We use it or we lose it, so the new world is not dissimilar to the hurly-burly around the Vatican in early sixteenth-century Rome where artists scrambled around the pit from which the Laocoön was being excavated, cutting one another to ribbons with insulting gibes and gestures that date back to Roman antiquity.

When I was living in Austin, Texas, in the 60s, the same conditions pertained, mitigated, I should note, by ganja benevolence. There was a rock-and-roll bar called the Vulcan Gas Company on Congress Avenue—its floor appropriately strewn with seeds, stems, rubbers, and syringes. Bands played four nights a week and slept in the room behind the bar. Artists, stoners, and tweekers hung around during the day, and the owners of the Vulcan, whose principal product, I suspect, was more agricultural than musical, fell upon the idea of recruiting local comic-book savants to design flyers for forthcoming bands like Shiva's Headband, 13th Floor Elevators, the Velvet Underground, Bubble Puppy, Blue Cheer, and Red Krayola.

The bands chugged into Austin in their trashed Econolines. A lot of them didn't have records out or even labels, so local ink-stained stoners made up the posters. Tattoo gothic and bubble letters were invented. Just as it happened in Ghana, a network of poster guys evolved who worked for the Vulcan in Austin, the Family Dog in Denver, and the Fillmore in San Francisco. My friend Jim Franklin, whose abstract paintings I exhibited in my art gallery, invented the legendary totem animal of slacker Austin: the noble, pitiful armadillo. Gilbert Shelton invented Wonder Wart-Hog in 1962 and the Furry Freak Brothers somewhat later. All these artists left a horde of defective superheroes and noir graphic novels in their wake.

When the Vulcan went legit, when the cops stopped sharing joints with us, and the bands had four-color graphics, the poster artists founded Zap Comix as a vehicle, first in Austin, then in San Francisco, and now in Paris where the work goes on at a steady pace. Tony Bell, before his untimely demise, moved from drawing rock-band posters to designing the Batboat for the first Batman movie. We were working on the Batboat one afternoon when Ken Kesey and his Merry Pranksters showed up in their bus. We did not like them. First, they were creaky geezers. Second, they made fun of the old ladies in the neighborhood who made us cookies. In our eyes, these nice ladies were only slightly older than the pranksters themselves. So, somewhere between Ginsberg and Hendrix, between Seattle and Austin, America had changed; a new brand of cosmopolitan tolerance had evolved that had something to do with cookies.

When the local becomes global without official accreditation, the world is really changing. The art that is held in museum custody can help but it can't change the flow. I have seen this happen again and again. We've all seen those science-fiction movies where time travelers flash back into some prehistoric jungle and someone drops a pistol or a fountain pen, and the travelers return to find a radically altered present. In the ghettos of global culture and out on its fringes, amazing things like this happen every day and always have. [Like the sneaker-lace design fad that started in Hong Kong and engulfed global teenage fashion in about three days.] This is the cosmopolitan way. No storehouses of vitrines can take it back to the way it was.

Cosmopolitanism is a time machine. It is the instrument out of which urban civilization grows—where one would never think to mow—until something is already transcending its *raison d'être*. The future arrives unannounced, and there is no refuge. We live on a cosmopolitan planet. Claude Lévi-Strauss was right. There is no such thing as primitivism, only anal-retentive curators and professors who have manicured "global art" down to the putting-green surfaces of provincial mainstream taste.

Something comes out of nothing and changes the future. Everything touches everyone eventually. A medieval Greek plowman strikes what he thinks is a rock in his field. It turns out to be a perfectly carved marble torso. The Byzantine world ends in this moment. Someone drops a can of spray paint in a squat in the Bronx. A black exile in Bangkok learns Thai fighting and brings it home to San Francisco. A Bruce Lee movie flickers on an old Sylvania TV, powered by a portable generator, in a dark village in the African bush. The kids start drawing flying Asians. Collectors, of course, prefer multiculti Chinoiserie, and Ghana has its own quality artists who make it, but I find the fenceless ephemeral cornucopia of Ghana's local art production a pretty good alternative. The vitrine we plunk down over the beaux arts is killing what it aspires to nurture, while Ghana is really starting to happen in the sunshine of absolute neglect.

1 Ernie Wolfe III [ed], *Extreme Canvas 2: The Golden Age of Hand-Painted Movie Posters from Ghana*, Kesho & Malaika Press, Los Angeles, CA, 2012.

First We Fight

MOST aspects of fighting in public cannot be written about, but I wanted to try. The fact that they *cannot* be written about is probably why we fight, why I want to try to write about it, and why we watch the fights. The outcome is in doubt, of course, as it is in all sports, but what does that say about the exotic, endorphin-fueled rush of pain and pleasure that accompanies ritualized hard training, except that it is real and that it transcends verbal expression. What does one say about the ease of camaraderie among one's peers and antagonists, about the comfort of stepping into the octagon—the one place in the world where you know exactly what to do?

How do you explain the odd gratitude you feel toward your opponent for simply being there and affording you the opportunity to focus, to be brave and fierce. Options like this are rare these days, so what does it say about the parts of fighting that are beyond knowing, like the tumbling, dreamy, virtually painless pain of really being hurt [a feeling I know because fighters share this experience with surfers], or about the sharp, short burst of exaltation that accompanies victory, then quickly fades and drives the need to fight again. All of these conditions exist, but they resist words. So things change.

Words were once a cure for fighting. Now fighting has become a cure for words because the words are lies. We all bear false witness, and just saying so seems insufficient to the scale of the lies. So I want to begin on a broader field with all the lonely arts that aspire to passion and precision, ferocity and nuance, where the risks are great, and the truest rewards reside in the state of one's heart, the moral necessity of one's opponents, and the sustenance of one's comrades. By writing about fighting across boundaries, I am joining a long line of writers better than I am: Ernest Hemingway, A. J. Liebling, Norman Mailer, F. X. Toole, and, most prominently in this case, Sam Sheridan, who began his quest for something real by studying painting at Harvard College and ended up as the bard of mixed martial arts.

Sheridan, at present, is the poet laureate of all those tattooed hard guys—"the disenfranchised, burning to test their manhood, angry at their father or the situation or *something*."[1] And there are connections between art and fighting. Many fighters and athletes end up as artists—eye-hand coordination being the link between them—but Sheridan's taking it the other way, from art to fighting, is a sign of the times—a measure of the anger and desperation that pervades the moment. So let me remind you that the last hundred years have been marked by the greatest flourishing of the temporal arts, fine and martial, in human history.

The mastery and popularity of these arts have increased exponentially. Now, more than ever, we esteem the arts in which years of training and failure redeem themselves in one incandescent moment of triumph—all those arts that are worth taking the trouble to see on the chance that something magic might transpire. So we are living through a great age of disciplined improvisation—of fighting, dancing, painting, acting, skateboarding, and all the rest—of making music, making people laugh, and making love.

Three primary cultural conditions have made this flourishing possible. First, for more than a century, we have been able to *record* those moments that, in previous centuries, melted into the air. The glories of bel canto singing, Edmund Kean's acting, and Vaslav Nijinsky's *Rite of Spring*, were totally unavailable a few seconds after they concluded. Now we have it all down to learn from. Second, we still have the right, in this culture, to put ourselves in harm's way, and the privilege of not dying in the effort. Finally, we live in a culture in which "the rules" are flexible and easily changeable when they become oppressive, divisive, or boring. This is a good thing, because any time two humans fight and both survive, the rules would be reason.

Recordings of the improvisational arts are critical. Without recordings of Louis Armstrong playing, Dixieland jazz would have persisted but as a kind of folk music. There would be no escalating platform of refinement and innovation—no Bix, no Diz, no Bird, no Trane, no Miles—and, in fact, no Jackson Pollock either. If there were no films of Jack Johnson and Jack Dempsey, we would still fight but without the innovations and refinements of Sugar Ray Robinson, Rocky Graziano, and Muhammad Ali. There would be no giants upon whose shoulders we might stand. The darker side of our access to representations resides in their ability to replace the real thing, as video games do, and to relocate our hearts in our thumbs—but there are always wild souls who want to make it real, so for many young fighters ultimate fighting replaces the video games of their youth. It incorporates moves that derive from those games, like the "levels"—the fight in the air and the fight on the ground.

The other dark consequence of recorded improvisation is that it offers a profusion of choices, and these choices create schools of fighting, music, dance, and art. These create coteries of specialists and imitators; they generate infinite divisions and subdivisions that present aspirants with self-limiting decisions: Sugar Ray, Bruce Lee, or Royce Gracie? Pollock, Andy Warhol, or Richard

Serra? Bix, Diz, or Chet? Conversations about these competing schools descend into adolescent arguments about "special powers," and at this point, the tradition of learning by watching and listening that once set us free becomes a kind of tyranny. Precision overwhelms passion, nuance overwhelms ferocity, and greed overwhelms justice.

And all we want is a fair fight—something just and beautiful—and this is where the privileges of democracy come into play. During the arguments that surrounded the ratification of the American constitution, there were those who argued against a permanent legislature. Why not just make some laws and enforce them forever? This sounds attractive for the moment, of course, but, for once, Alexander Hamilton and Thomas Jefferson agreed: We need lawmakers because we always need new rules. The needs and desires of commercial cultures change. The rule that liberates us today may easily imprison us tomorrow. The rule that unites us today may easily divide us tomorrow, so the rules change, and, in the process, they free us from tyranny, divide us according to our tastes, and reunite us according to our desires in earnest.

The mixed martial arts have done something more radical. They have unified ancient traditions of fighting and broken down divisions that have roots in the gene pools of a thousand cultures: in the folk histories of the Greek and Roman West, of the Gothic North, in the traditions of China, Japan, and Thailand. The fact that all of these rich disciplines with deep local roots could mix and proliferate worldwide is a testament to the combative appetite of mercantile capitalism. The fact that all these disciplines could come together in mixed martial arts is a tribute to the creative power of cosmopolitanism, to the forces of globalism at their best, and to the challenges that face an autumnal America smoldering with social anger.

So people are getting ready for something, they know not what or for how long. As a consequence, Ultimate Fighting is ultimate not because it lacks rules. It is ultimate because it lacks respite. It goes on in nonstop five-minute rounds [three or five of them] until a fighter is knocked out or submits by "tapping out." So it is not the danger and cruelty of the conflict that makes it ultimate but the outrageous demands it places on the body of the fighter. There *are* rules, in fact, thirty-one of them, written by my friend Lorenzo Fertitta and his board and designed to make death, concussion, and bone injury less likely. Head butting, eye gouging, fish hooking, biting, hair pulling, cursing, spitting, stomping, spiking, clawing, and pinching are verboten. Attacks to the groin, the throat, the fingers, and toes are verboten; strikes to the back of the head and to the spine are forbidden.

There are rules that accommodate the differing conditions of the fight, fighting standing or fighting on the ground. There are rules that eliminate the false theater of wrestling [no holding to the enclosure; no throwing your opponent out of the enclosure]. The holds and blows that will kill if not rehearsed and expected [as they are in wrestling] are banned. There are rules that eliminate the leisurely politesse of boxing: no broken clinches or standing eights, none of the little rest stops that relax the demands of combat on the body. There are also built-in restraints. The arm and leg holds that will break an arm or a leg if executed decisively are applied gradually to create submissions and are punished if they are not. The light gloves that allow grappling also encourage restraint in blows to the head [the head being harder than the hand in every case]. The possibility of grabbing mitigates the boxing and karate moves that require radical extension of the arms or the legs. This also lessens, although it does not eliminate, the advantage of reach.

In the end then, we have something we might call a fair fight of immense complexity, one that favors the survival of the fittest, a fight that teaches us things we never quite realized about the lives we live. To take an instance: when I first began watching Ultimate

Fighting in Las Vegas, I thought the fight on the ground was boring. Gradually it revealed itself to me in all its subtle urgency. One night, I realized that, like *Glengarry Glen Ross*, the fight on the ground is the true metaphor of how we live today. Down at the office, the university, or the plant, we rarely have the opportunity to stand up and punch it out. On the job, in the bureaucracy, we grapple forever on the ground, seeking tiny advantages, bits of leverage, and the occasional clean shot. Herein lies the true satisfaction of the standing knockout.

So why fight this kind of fight now? I attribute it to the enormous tectonic forces alive in America today, where we have never been so safe and in so much peril. We live in a filigree of perfectly interconnected safety nets with helmet laws, seat belts, infant seating, low cholesterol, no-smoking signs, playdates, cell phones, and e-mail. All this coddles people trying to work on the precipice of absolute disaster. One merger, one outsourced job, one bad decision, one deceptive mortgage, one religious idiot, one accident, one gun nut or illness, and we are falling forever, and we can't even scream lest we disturb the peace. So you ask: Why fight? I say, Why not? Don't we need a little space, an octagon, perhaps, where no self-serving lies need be spoken, where we know exactly what's going down?

1 Sam Sheridan, *A Fighter's Heart: One Man's Journey through the World of Fighting*, Atlantic Monthly Press, New York, NY, 2007.

Formalism

I SAW my first Chinese opera in the early 1970s, in Manhattan, on a whim, because a Blue Öyster Cult concert had been canceled. I loved the whole thing. The performers were beautiful. The makeup was beautiful. The costumes made Liberace look like Dick Cheney, and the music sounded like Blue Öyster Cult falling down stairs. I didn't understand anything, but I walked out of the theater very excited. I told my companion that if I saw four more Chinese operas, knowing nothing more than I did then, I could tell which was the best one, once I identified the parts. Four was optimistic. There are 360 regional forms of Chinese opera, according to one playbill I read, and they can only be understood against the backdrop of Chinese history, so, in my case, it took six or seven. I saw my last Chinese opera in April 2006 at La MaMa down on 4th Street, *The Dragon-Princess and the Scholar*.

I still knew nothing beyond my experience of seeing six or seven performances, but even so, in 2006, I could feel the shape of the piece, the logic of the spectacle. I recognized infelicities and corners cut. I reveled in bravura moments and exquisite details, and, most critically, I felt in tune with the predominantly Asian audience, most of whom, I suspected, were hardcore New Yorkers no more erudite about the 360 forms than I. This was important to me because, during the period of my Chinese Opera Project, modernists like Picasso and Degas were being called to the bar for "plundering" Asian and African sources and exploiting the cultural integrity of these sources. This tribal proposition, as I pointed out at the time, neglects the fact that Velázquez and Ribera lived in the wake of a Moorish culture. Spain was awash in North African influences and that the French Rococo, thanks to plantations in Indochina, was inundated by Oriental tropes, thus an Oriental predisposition was already part of being French. Africa was already a part of being Spanish. Scolding Picasso for grooving on Yoruba artifacts and degrading Degas for his Oriental tropes, is like indicting me for speaking English instead of Zuni.

The fatwa against cultural borrowing, however, was only a tactical feint. My real adversary was the escalating jihad against formalism in contemporary art criticism. At that time, professors were attacking formalism at the very moment that iconic theorists like Jacques Derrida, Noam Chomsky, and Gilles Deleuze were arguing in its defense. This seemed a willful turning away from difficulty—as if the American art world, given the chance to watch Michelangelo Antonioni's *Red Desert*, had opted for Elvis Presley's *Blue Hawaii*. So I started calling myself a formalist critic because everyone was calling Clement Greenberg a formalist critic. He wasn't. He never really addressed the shape of anything and was, I suspect, color-blind. He was a literate Marxist, so, obviously, the formalist job was still open.

When people asked me why I was embracing the f-word, I would ask them this: "When Jacques Derrida asserts that there is no meaning outside the text, do you think it's a fact or a problem? If you think it's a fact, you're a formalist. If you think it's a 'problem' that might be *fixed*, you are a reactionary idealist." I would always remind my inquisitors that human beings do not express themselves telepathically. Everything goes out into the physical world in tangible patterns. It comes back in through our hard-wired capacity to detect patterns and report any anomalies to our consciousness through blips or floods of emotion. So a lot comes in of which we are not consciously aware that just stays in storage, at the ready, awaiting its cue. Chomsky proposes that human beings express themselves by manipulating a finite vocabulary of tangible signs through a finite number of transformations to create an infinite array of utterances.

These patterns are internally meaningful—color to color, word to word, mark to mark, noise to noise. Their relationship to the world beyond is always flimsy because, as Deleuze argues, the meaning and reference that we derive from any utterance or text is inextricable from the tangible "logic of sensation" that governs our expression and perception of it. How else could we enjoy the atmospheric nonsense of Lewis Carroll's "Jabberwocky," which is rife with hints but otherwise devoid of real-world referents?

My first conscious experience with the logic of sensation took place in the Ransom Library at the University of Texas in Austin where I sat, wearing white gloves, in a beige carrel and read a fair copy manuscript of D. H. Lawrence's *Women in Love* straight through, foolscap sheet by foolscap sheet. By the time I had finished, the steady, curving logic of Lawrence's insistent handwriting [no mark outs, no interlinear revisions] had so totally infected the narrative that, even today, I can't look at a printed page of *Women in Love* without feeling the terrible absence of Lawrence's brown cursive, drawn across a page nearly a century ago. This experience [especially with the white gloves], contributed to my becoming an art critic and set me off in search of the intimate bang of *The Dragon-Princess and the Scholar*, which I enjoyed as a child delights in the *Jabberwocky*.

If Chomsky's overarching theory is anywhere near right [and he is wrong sometimes, about personal pronouns] the whole of human utterance can be experienced without translation—if we can identify the finite number of tangible "parts" in an expression.

Formalists analyze events that have already happened. They don't teach us how to "enjoy" art. They investigate the consequences of parts [words, notes, colors] that usually remain un-recognized to us. If we tease out the finite sums of each part and the proportion of each part to another, we are on our way to having a shape. When we learn the curves—the frequencies with which the parts and their redundancies occur—we have some sense of its various tempos. [In literature phonemes, go faster than sentences.] When we know enough about the genre of expression to recognize the parts and frequencies that *don't* occur, we know a great deal.

The problem is that most critics are more fluent in philosophy than arithmetic, Boolean algebra, and calculus, but the numbers are there. We usually know them before we even count, but we *should* count. The triumphant formalist study of music, I should note, is Leonard Meyer's *The Rhythmic Structure of Music*. To analyze a literary text, we should begin with a total vocabulary—a list of units and sums of their redundancies. We should know how many parts are important—the proper nouns, verbs, phonemes, consonants, tenses, adverbs, adjectives, pronouns, demonstratives, and their redundancies. If we know what doesn't occur and the frequencies at which the parts that do occur occur, we have a great deal of applicable information about the conformation of the object's vocabulary.

If we learn the frequency at which new information is fed into the work, we have another usable curve. A text with mostly "new" words is virtually unreadable, so the curve of new words invariably flattens then rises at the volta. To cite a couple of instances: The proportion and redundancy of adverbs and adjectives should remind us that even their *appearance* in literary prose is problematic, that synonyms of any sort rarely appear in memorable writing except as jokes. We learn that a flat line of sentence lengths is euphonic suicide. We learn that the redundancy of, say, Hemingway's prose, improves its velocity.

We learn that his routinely incorrect usage of "which" over "that" makes his art more eloquent by suppressing subordination.

Clement Greenberg always insisted that one's sense of a work's quality, virtue, or intensity is as instantaneous as the mind's ability to sense patterns and to infer their "on-purpose-ness" without knowing that purpose. For once, I agree with Clement. We can processes massive arrays of patterns [as in a Chinese opera], without being able to sort them out, define them, isolate them, or even identify them. This ignorance does not impair their effectiveness, however. Stochastic patterns and sequences of any sort elicit responses. Total ignorance of thoroughbreds does not mitigate the pleasures of the horse race, although eventually one learns that art, music, and literature are founded on obbligatos of redundancy and moments of eccentricity. These make the arts memorable. They live in memory. Sorting out the parts that make the whole is what formalism does. In music we start with the parts and adduce the whole; in art we start with the whole and adduce the parts to our satisfaction.

In art criticism and music criticism, there is no dictionary, and in literary prose there shouldn't be. The virtue of not having a dictionary is that patterns present themselves to us that are unaccounted for in "correct" readings, and this increases the works' longevity, because all expressions contain secondary and tertiary patterns that contribute to the work's conscious purpose, but the parts can change. First we love the picture, then we love the paint, then we love the arrangement. The primary virtue of formalism is that it allows you to see and hear patterns that were not put there—that only ended there as a side effect of some other pattern more urgently desired by the artist. Formalist readings can reverse their hierarchy. Because of this, Jackson Pollock could look at Thomas Hart Benton's folksy murals in Jefferson City, Missouri, upon which he was assisting, and see *Autumn Rhythm* [1950]. Jerome Robbins could look at *Autumn Rhythm* and see a dance.

Sadly, the attacks against formalism in the early 70s had little to do with fact or philosophy. The jihad was a radical maneuver designed to "liberalartsify" contemporary art. Professors needed a way of talking about contemporary art that was adapted to their *Clockwork Orange* [eyes-clamped-open] classroom procedures. They needed something to say while student brains were washed with "art history." In these chambers of horror, children were coerced into looking at pictures of pictures they did not care about and to which they did not respond. Pictures of art provided the texts. Professors provided the dictionary. This evil practice has been long since discontinued, I'm sure, but I want to emphasize the fact that formalism doesn't do dictionary, darling; it doesn't do answers; it doesn't do pictures of art; and it doesn't do coerced looking. Formalism speculates on the intensity and possible longevity of tangible art that elicits an instantaneous visual or emotional confirmation.

We try to isolate the critical frequencies, ask the right questions, and never gain knowledge or truth. Sometimes, we come up with little Aesopian morals, but nothing major. Jasper Johns's flag suggests that its value derives from the people who salute it, not from the man who made it. Richard Serra's work reminds us that we never stand alone, that we must lean against the world, against one another, or curve to abeyance to the god of gravity. My favorite moral is found in Joan Mitchell's painting. Joan reminds us that she can do it and we can't. She is the Monica Vitti of art, pure neurosis. So formalism doesn't do answers because answers, would conclude the endless dance of inquiries that keeps the work alive.

I remember looking at Jasper Johns's *Target with Faces* [1955] in his retrospective at the Museum of Modern Art in New York thinking that a half-century of intelligent speculation had brought us no closer to decoding its mysteries—and that this didn't matter at all. It had been a long romance, and we always had Paris, or wherever Jasper's *Target* first became the target of our gaze. This is a testament to Johns as an artist but also a reminder that art leaves questions unanswered, and I could not help but feel, standing there in the MOMA, that we might do well to stop mooning over the targets for a while and let them freshen up. Then, one day in the future, in Brussels or Newport Beach, some youngster might come upon them, and the song would begin again. That mysterious aura of on-purpose-ness would take hold, and off we go into the sunset.

So formalism begins with an instantaneous sense of alien, patterned complexity. We stand before a work of art with no hope of understanding it and no choice but to try. We reenact the primal cosmopolitan moment—the first time a human being stood face to face with a stranger from a strange place with a strange language, "sizing things up" without a dictionary. I met my first genuine strangers of this sort in the 1960s, when I had the benefit of taking courses from the great writer Jorge Luis Borges, the new journalist Tom Wolfe, the French avant gardiste Nathalie Sarraute, and the great classicist Bill Arrowsmith. I don't remember a word they said. I remember that Borges wore a cape and fedora, that Wolfe was a smartass, and Arrowsmith a show-off. I remember that Nathalie Sarraute had a mind as exquisite and strange as a Chinese opera. What I *learned* from these strangers was something like what I learned from D. H. Lawrence's manuscript. I learned just *exactly* how high eloquence manifests itself, what it feels like to be around, how it moves in its mortality. This turned out to be a good thing to know.

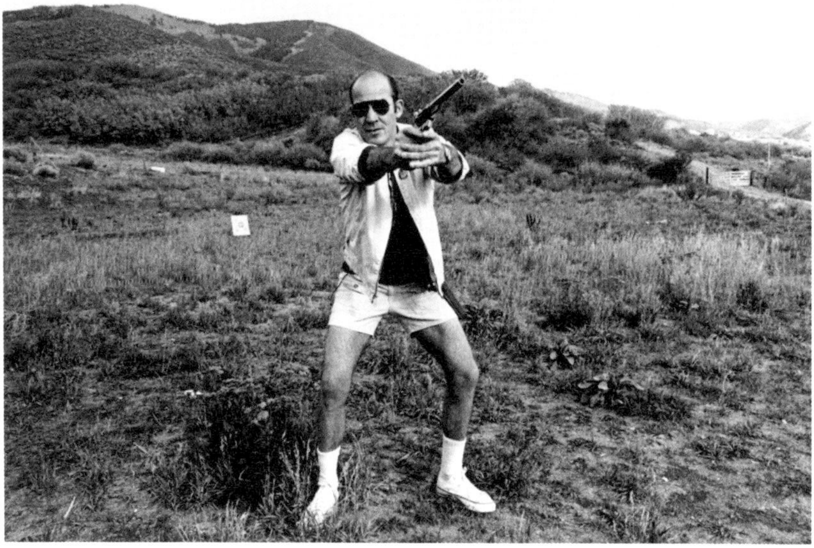

Hunter S. Thompson, c.1976

Fear and Loathing Goes to Hell

HUNTER S. THOMPSON and I were professional acquaintances for about twenty years. Along with Nick Tosches, James Walcott, Grover Lewis, Lester Bangs, Robert Christgau, John Morthland, Chet Flippo, and other speedy typists, we were what they used to call "new journalists"—freestyle purveyors of "cultural reportage." We wrote for the magazines with the shelf life of milk. We wrote about subjects with the shelf life of milk. We prowled the same airports and lived the same poorly regulated, profligate lives. Hunter S., as it turned out, became famous for his profligacy. Not one of us begrudged him his fame. The toxicity of lurid fame was our one true subject, and, as Bangs put it, our job was to report back to the kids in Omaha about the dead girl in the lobby. Hunter, like all of us, had seen blood splashed on the curtains, and if Hunter wanted to be Mick Jagger, he was welcome to it. And he had a right, because Hunter Thompson was a very good writer, a wonderful writer, in fact, for a one-trick pony. He did lyric bile, fear, loathing, and rabid denunciation without much else in his quiver.

Given the times, of course, lyric bile was usually sufficient, but, as a writer and a person, Hunter was never in a place you wanted to be. It was no fun, and Hunter himself, whose life was redolent with opportunities for fun, never seemed to be having any unless he was laying waste to something or someone. While you were chatting up the Valkyrie in the fuzzy, scoop-neck sweater that was barely containing her awesome, quivering breasts, Hunter was spraying the room with a fire extinguisher. This sort of jackass intervention was extremely exasperating. Eventually, it became sad or disgusting, depending on your generosity.

So if we, his fellow scribblers, begrudged Hunter anything, it was not his lifestyle. It was writing *about* that lifestyle and, in the process, outing of *our* lifestyles by telling people what we were doing. There are some creatures who like to dance but do not like the light, and, for nearly a decade, before Hunter became a "name"—before "rock writer" became a part you played in the alley behind some concert hall—we were invisible, a tribe of happy, insatiable shadows on the loose. We had all the perks of fame and none of the grief. We got the planes, the limos, the hotels, the good money, and the backstage passes. We got the free cocaine, the speed, the smack, and the barbits. We got the buffet, the tour jackets, the top-floor balconies, and the beautiful girls [more of these than you can possibly imagine], whom we were privileged to select after the band but before the roadies. Best of all, we got to write about music, to live in a bubble of music, and not surprisingly, music was a subject that never aroused Hunter Thompson's passion. Hunter liked rich folks. If they were rich musicians, fine. He liked power players, Johnny Depp, race-car drivers, gun nuts, Hells Angels, and politicians.

Hunter wanted to be the Sheriff of Aspen. We wanted to be Robin Hood's merry men. Being an inconspicuous merry man meant that when you were finally sated and demented, having sampled the spicy gruel of American celebrity, you could, if you wanted to, put on a Lakers cap, change your jacket, and stroll away, just disappear into the night. Jimmy Page couldn't do this. He had to buy a castle. So, when Hunter himself finally disappeared, when he shot himself, my first reaction was that it might have been slightly more respectful of the living had Hunter, who loved explosions, just strolled away into the woods and blown himself into slightly smaller bits. He chose otherwise, and in the days after he died, a couple of journalists called for quotes. I told them that I liked Hunter as much as a lover could like a hater, from which I hoped they could infer that I meant "not very much."

I did respect the dude, however, so, in his wake, I reread *Fear and Loathing in Las Vegas*. I found it as narcissistic now as it was then. Laying the book aside, I found myself, for the first time, feeling sympathy for Johnny Depp. My first beef with the book is that nothing happens in it that requires the city of Las Vegas. There's no gambling. There are no money rolls, no whales, no whores, no crap tables, no showgirls, and no scumbag hustlers. Rereading the book now, at home in Las Vegas, it feels as if Hunter was simply not up to sharing the stage with the local color, no matter how vivid he felt. There is, however, a lot of desert highway in Hunter's book, a lot of blistering, Mojave, which Hunter mistakes for the landscape of the American soul. This is *way* too Hollywood to me. I am a formalist. I love the Mojave, and there are more desolate places in Providence, Rhode Island.

At any rate, the events in *Fear and Loathing in Las Vegas* could have taken place in any American city during the 1970s—and they did, because there were no *places* then, just blur and drift—hard-cash transactions, night flights, smoking sections, and no airport security. One night in the 70s, I climbed on a little plane to fly from Denver to Aspen. I noticed a songwriter friend of mine curled up in a front row. I said, "Hey dude, nice to see you." He made a tiny little wave and said softly, "Excuse my manners, man, but I'm just about to die." I nodded in sympathy and walked past him into the dark plane—quite unaware that he was, in fact, just about to die—remembering an afternoon in New York when I traded Lowell George's phone number to a girl in the songwriter's entourage for a bag of blow. Not my finest hour, but even so, the girl just wanted to fuck Lowell. So what. That night on the plane, I ended up in the back row with two ski bunnies, sharing bumps to the shivering hum of the props in the cold air. When we landed in Aspen, a guy in a chauffeur's uniform came on board. He lifted my friend out of his seat and carried him down to a limo that was waiting on the tarmac. I waved goodbye to the receding taillights, then set off into the swirling midnight snow after the ski bunnies.

That was the 70s—limos, homos, bimbos, resort communities, and cavernous stadiums—the whole culture in a giant, Technicolor Cuisinart, whipping by, and I did love it so. Thinking back now, I can't help but feel that Hunter missed a lot of the stagy grandeur or had no taste for it. He never seemed to have much use for groupies or homosexuals like my songwriter friend, or even for casual romance. I did meet a porn star friend of Hunter's one night at a dinner in Vail. Her name was Sharon Mitchell. She was a tall, bright, handsome woman who made wonderful, squirmy sex on film. She now runs an AIDS clinic in Los Angeles for many of her ex-colleagues. Hunter treated her with the sullen disdain you might expect from a boho snob—a demeanor that was perfectly inline with his hysterical loathing for working stiffs and service personnel. This, I should note, remains inexplicable to me to this day. In Hunter's Vegas book, the waiter at the Polo Lounge is a dwarf; the store clerk is a mongoloid; the room service waiter is a reptile; the lady at check-in is a gorgon, and I hate this. Savaging the weak is not funny, and as a matter of journalistic practice, these working stiffs are invariably the sources from whom you get the story, because Lou Reed, for all his confrontational candor, is not going to share with a journalist his late-night room service order for K-Y Jelly.

So, even now, *Fear and Loathing in Las Vegas* feels feverish, famished by amphetamines, and genuinely afraid of itself. In this book, as elsewhere, one gets the sense that Hunter never really found his place, that he never got over the la-di-da South, the Derby Cocktail Soiree, the Tea Dance, and the strut of southern manhood. The manners were gone, of course, but the raw, hot, dirt plantation sense of Faulknerian empowerment remained. One night at a wedding in New Orleans, a cultured woman from Thompson's part of the South told me how easily she could imagine Hunter a hundred years ago as a Civil War dandy, in his whalebone corset, his tailored uniform, his riding crop, and silver flask—and his dueling pistols, of course, always at the ready to defend his "honor."

I could never make that leap, but I could see the puritan do-gooder with a gun, and I can't help feeling the bleak shadow of puritan revenge in Thompson's Vegas adventures. During the narrative, the author describes himself committing a whole cornucopia of transgressions and felonies. He drives recklessly, wrecks cars, totes guns, drops acid, snorts coke, sniffs ether, and smokes ganja. He insults civilians, walks checks, abandons rentals, and dodges tabs at fancy hotels. All of these Mister Toad behaviors, I shamefully admit, were pretty much *de rigueur* for "cultural reporters" in those years. The strange thing is that, for all the crime and bad manners, for all the macho self-aggrandizement, there is no *sin* in Hunter's Sin City—no fucking, to be blunt, not even a blow job and, minus these accoutrements, Hunter's Vegas tastes like sucking pennies.

In fact, there is no sex and not much sexy in any of Hunter S. Thompson's writings, no encounters with whores, homos, bimbos, ex-wives, divorcees, barmaids, personal assistants, editors, or members of the wait staff, and these glaring omissions profoundly distort the milieu he purports to portray. In truth, Hunter's writing repudiates the primary vibe of the zeitgeist, because the post-flower-child 70s, I can assure you, were very, very sexy—even sexier at night—and a whole lot sexier in Las Vegas.

In those days, one did not go out on the road with Aerosmith or even Hubert Humphrey to huff glue with celebrities. "Face time" is a contemporary kink. You went out there to bathe in the dazzled libido of shiny America—to promenade down glimmering streets with crazy girls in torn T-shirts under a blood-red sky—but not Hunter S. Thompson. Hunter hated it all, and his suicidal hatred of the body, I suspect, made him the bard of choice for looky-no-touchy, *Less than Zero* America—the era of post-sex-global-fury—the age of AIDS and herpes, silicone, and Botox. This makes Thompson prescient, I guess [like Jeff Skilling of Enron, *avant la lettre*], arrogant, wasted, drooling, and snarling at the waiter.

Oh my, what a life!

American Cool

DURING the 1970s, when I was a tyro, every new work of art that I found refreshingly self-evident was immediately dubbed "cool and ironic" by someone important. I remember a "cool and ironic" Bridget Riley, an Andy Warhol, a Lynda Benglis, a Richard Tuttle, a John McCracken, and a Barry Le Va. None of them were "cool and ironic," and they had nothing in common beyond the possibility that they might not *be* ironic, but these were the halcyon days of Poststructuralism. Art was either what it appeared to be or the opposite of what it appeared to be. Under this regimen, "cool and ironic" became a preemptive catchphrase for not believing your eyes, and the damage it wrought has been incalculable.

Today, I suspect that the catchphrase "cool and ironic" papers over a catastrophic abyss in the transatlantic art culture that came into being during 60s and 70s, because, for Europeans, irony is more than a rhetorical figure, it is a justifiable mode of deflection and defense. For Americans, cool is more than a rhetorical figure; it is an official form of democratic cultural politesse. This is distressing because, if the visual cultures of New York, Berlin, Milan, Los Angeles, Paris, and London could be intellectually united under the auspices of "cool and ironic," we would have a clear field of play. They are *not* compatible, however, nor are the cultures that "cool and ironic" purported to unite. [Over dinner one night, Bob Hughes informed me that I could never get drunk enough to be an Englishman. He was right, but then he shrank back from a nice spoon of flake.]

So, generally speaking, Europeans are historically accustomed to serving many masters. I have known senior Europeans who have lived in Belgium, France, and Germany without leaving the house—depending on the day of the week—so, of necessity, they do irony very well. Some brand of repression is presumed. Sigmund Freud, Karl Marx, Bertolt Brecht, Marcel Duchamp, and Francis Picabia are sublime ironists, counterintuitive ghosts with vague secrets and opaque agendas. Except for Alain Robbe-Grillet, Charles Lamb, and Bridget Riley, Europeans just don't get cool. My friend Peter Schjeldahl assures me that not one European understands Roy Lichtenstein's *Whaam!* [1963] that hangs at the Tate Modern. "They think it's about war," the artist told me later. "It's about love at first sight."

The option of being cool or ironic has crossed the Atlantic, of course, but the world still flies apart because cool and irony are contraindicated means to the same end. They each enable us to speak our minds while maintaining a small margin of deniability. When we use irony, we suppress the intellectual *sense* of what we say. When we use cool, we suppress the *urgency* of what we mean. By simultaneously suppressing urgency and subverting sense, we devolve into lame sarcasm. We recreate the gay patois of my parents' generation. We speak in italics, featherlight and ever so faintly. "That Gary Cooper is so *intellectual*."

"Contextual irony" is the term that appears most often in critical writing of this period. This worked one time only. When Warhol's Marilyns were hung in the hallowed galleries of the Whitney Museum of American Art, hallowedness perished. Today, the artistic desecration of vestigial hallowedness is embarrassing for everyone—although Vanessa Beecroft stirred up some geriatric chubbies with her naked girls at the Guggenheim. Today, "cool" and "irony" mean *nothing at all*, nor does "flatness," "resistance," "diversity," "transgressive," "interrogate," or any of the other catchphrases that pepper art publications.

I'm embarrassed just typing the words, because words are important to me, and I intend to take them seriously one last time. After this, I promise, just italics and charm, and everything will be *so intellectual*. But, just for a moment, presume that I am usually right about potential longevity of art. I have an art critic's skill set—good eyes, eidetic memory, proper languages, catholic taste, and a long familiarity with the artists and the works in question. Presume further that I am familiar with the history of Classical rhetoric. Along with Quintilian and many other writers, I insist that evidence must exist for any work to bear the attribution of irony, and none of the works I have mentioned meet that criteria, so why bother dubbing cool works ironic when they can pass for either.

An ironic statement asserts an altogether antagonistic meaning than it appears to be offering by some *identifiable sign*. In bureaucratic cultures where there is no free expression, irony is required to elude the wrath of one's betters. Jonathan Swift's *A Modest Proposal* argues that cooking and consuming Irish babies would solve the Irish population problem and the famine to boot. This is neither modest nor a proposal. It is ironic. The dissonance between the tea and crumpets *mise-en-scène* and the heroic diction of Alexander Pope's *The Rape of the Lock* brews up a deliciously ironic cocktail.

Cool is something altogether different. It is the act of being *seen* being oneself. It is theater without drama, demonstration without pleading, distinction without discrimination, and dissent without violence. For those of us who live in a world bereft of our betters amidst a surfeit of free expression, cool is a valuable resource. Cool people are not noisy or boring. They eschew footnotes and asseveration. Expressive flailing is verboten. You simply declare some specific truth to be self-evident on one's own authority, and the music flows out like a Miles Davis solo. You amaze your peers by investing the evangelical urgency of your eccentric opinions with sotto voce buoyancy, killing them softly.

They can still get you, though, because professors, evidently, harbor secret powers. One night in New York, after a talk about California art, I actually confronted a "cool and ironic" professor-critic, now dead, with the lunacy of his position on McCracken. His answer was that McCracken made *dead, silent things* that could still be enriched by irony in the professor's elevated historical consciousness of late-capitalist production. This act of Marxist ventriloquism, he argued, could make McCracken's work useful to students who, being students, will happily use a lie to make an A. So words still have their coded uses.

Years ago, I was introduced before delivering a university lecture. My appointed introducer described my life's labor as "a personal testament" and a "cool, ironic critique of contemporary culture." I delivered my lecture anyway, although, in academic parlance, "personal testament" and "cool and ironic critique" mean "Don't trust this guy—the wine is corked." Irony in art, of course, precludes irony in diction, so before I said a word, my host had robbed my case of all general urgency. He had preempted the public relevance of my remarks and prepared the ground for his own post-lecture seminar during which everything he agreed with was banal, and anything he disagreed with was naïve.

So I lost and the institution won, but what did they win? Dog biscuits? More growling time in the manger? Had I been quick enough as I mounted the podium, I should have announced that, yes, I was trying to be cool: because cool is the prevailing manner of democratic politesse. But really, kids, who would resort to *irony* in Iowa City? The university boasts a writers' workshop with ironists thick on the ground. Irony presumes repression, and presuming repression where none exists makes you look like a clown. Also why should anyone be *personal* in *Iowa City*? Again, they *have* a writers' workshop to do this work, and I am not a personal person.

More to the point, you are actually *invited* to universities to be sneered at and babysit students in the dead of winter. This public service has no celebrity perks and doesn't pay diddly, so one doesn't solicit speaking gigs. One responds to invitations because one should. And I always try to tell the truth. I try to be cool. I don't even know how to *do* irony, and no critic has had need of it since Leigh Hunt, who was incapable of it. Hunt *was* sent to poet's prison for dissing the Prince of Wales. Lord Byron visited him in the pokey and brought along some wine. They played cards and talked of poesy.

In the absence of princes and Wales, there is no punishment for naughty lecturers in the United States beyond resentment. It's hard to demote someone without a job, to bankrupt someone with no money, or to steal power from someone without any, although I could, I suppose, be banished. This would deny me the pleasure of staring out a sealed window into the eternal snow in a blonde motel room at a Best Western, then bundling up and bouncing off through the snowstorm in some undergraduate's Volkswagen for cheap Thai food with the junior faculty. Once banished, I would be forced to play cards in gaudy casinos all weekend, drink free drinks, and smoke cigarettes, so, trust me, I am *never* ironic.

So the villain in my story is the loveless marriage between art and the "liberal arts." If this were a happy union, Cambridge, Mass, would be Paris in the 20s. Unfortunately art is not a liberal art. It does not constitute a body of knowledge in any traditional sense. It has scrap heaps of theories and oodles of information but no true proof, internal conformation, dictionary, or stable contextual reference. In class, I could tell my students who made something, when it was made it, where it was made, and what it's made from. I could share my knowledge of local iconography, and tell some jolly historical anecdotes. Then I would have to remind my students that Ellsworth Kelly's oeuvre arises out of an odd triangle created by a woman's shoulder in a sweater in a painting by Max Beckmann, so forget about everything I just said. QED.

Even so, we should look at any art that is more interesting than the wall on which it hangs. We may read paintings, too, if we wish, but there is no urgent need of it. For the last thirty years, however, in the aftermath of the liberal-arts putsch, professors really do need theoretical space eaters to fill up the hours. The whole deconstructive schlimazel is tailored to help them force-feed images to unwilling captives with the clock ticking. So what is a professor to say about Cy Twombly? I would say: "Well kids, Cy is cool. He can do this, and you can't with your crippled little hands." A sequence of Twombly images would pass in silence, during which students might have some ideas of their own.

That would be that. And *what*'s that? Twenty seconds in a long class. As a consequence, the coolest, silent art of the last century goes untaught or misconstrued, and this amounts to willful academic suppression. I have always felt that great art aspires to a kind of musical silence—in John Cage's sense of bounded quiet—and I have spent my career struggling for words to address silent art, because it is my taste and because the effort exerts stress on my critical language. Sadly, this improves the prose, but not always the art.

Here is the problem: the traditional democratic politesse of American art abjures any sign of "repression," and "superiority." Progressive critics deem this brand of decorum in American art "complacent." My English friend Jeremy Gilbert Rolfe once characterized Abstract Expressionism as abstract repressionism, and he was not far wrong. American art *is* complacent. Even the work of Jackson Pollock can pass for the production of a superior tapestry designer with a great wrist. Harold Rosenberg called it "apocalyptic wallpaper," and *he* was not far wrong. Read Clement Greenberg bestowing Kenneth Noland [the most complacent artist in the *beau monde*] with a red flag for his buttonhole, and you get the idea.

George Washington, however, was certifiably cool, as was Charles S. Peirce, Henry James, Gertrude Stein, Warhol, and Kelly. They embody their beliefs in public while declining to plead them. In this particular sense, cool is a peculiarly American virtue. It is the manner *de jour* of jazzmen, power forwards, jefes, and California painters. Wearing dark shades is an African inheritance. They are the icons of cool. Cool people even wear shades indoors. The fate of cool American art, after its apotheosis in the 60s, may be attributed mostly to fashion, of course, but it owes something to the institutional triumph of Walter Benjamin's warm rabbinical-romanticism and a Marxist sociology that is only marginally concerned with physical objects, totally unconcerned with empirical correlatives, and deeply obsessed with a culture damned by irony, angst, repression, spectacle, false consciousness, and *mauvaise foi*.

The classical exemplum of cool comes from a passage in Cicero's *De Oratore*. The author declares that he can enter the Forum at its far end, observe a speaker on the podium from that distance [over a hundred yards], and without hearing a word, ascertain the effectiveness of the speaker and the equity of his case. From this example, Cicero derives his concept of the orator who need not speak at all, who need only mount the dais to make the quality of his virtue and his case visible through the presence of his body. The deep historical link between classical rhetoric and Renaissance painting [in both its design and pantomime] resides in this ideal of the orator as a silent object of virtue. In Christian times, this idea of visible virtue was reconstituted as a condition of grace, but it remains the very emblem of cool—of that which need only be seen to be believed.

To make the American connection with cool more emphatic, I should note that Washington, in his time, was recognized as the historical embodiment of Cicero's oratorical ideal. His writings and speeches are Senecan and straightforward, the furthest thing from brilliant. His generalship was fierce, brave, and intelligent. His presidency was studious and professional, notable mostly for the power he refused, the powers he limited, and the alliances he didn't make. He gave away most of the power he had been granted, because the crown is not yours until you can refuse it.

And yet, for the citizens of that tiny republic on the edge of the Atlantic, and, for all the brilliant, erratic lawyers, farmers, and adventurers who constituted its revolutionary cabal, he was the one indispensable creature, and he didn't really stand *for* anything. He simply stood—the embodiment of everything the republic might be. Accounts of Washington's power and influence always begin with his carriage; the way he stood, sat, walked, or rode. Washington's ease in the saddle became a metaphor for the ease with which he settled disputes. More surprising to moderns, accounts of Washington's physical graces never presumed them to be cosmetic. They were presumed to be embodiments of republican virtue, and Washington never did or said anything to disabuse anyone of this notion.

Because of our respect for his triumph, however, not nearly enough is made of Washington's predisposition to take risks, of his flashes violent anger at the card table or on the battlefield. Ferocity and daring are important attributes for a rebel general, and they clarify the means through which Washington became himself. Otherwise, there were no perfidies, hypocrisies, vendettas, secret vices, or outstanding debts to sully the image because Washington was that man—the incarnation of virtue, invulnerable to tell-all gossip, because there was nothing to tell beyond the remembrances of those who saw him ride.

Consider Washington's deportment at the Second Continental

Congress, which could never have been assembled without his guaranteed presence. Throughout the deliberations, the shouting and wrangling, the nitpicking and backbiting, Washington sat with hands in his lap and his legs crossed, saying little to nothing. Occasionally, when the debate became especially heated or seemed to divagate from its purposes, Washington would shift his weight in his chair and cross his legs the other way. At that moment, as if he had turned the tiller on the Ship of State, the debate would take a new direction. That, my friends, is cool and the very emblem of the way cool art functions in a secular society. It sits there, or hangs there, a seamless, candid incarnation of recognizable power investing our anxious quarrels with decorum. [It seems inappropriate, somehow, to shout in the presence of a floating, glowing Robert Irwin disc.]

The epitome of Washington's cool was his serious reluctance to run for a second term. He was ultimately persuaded to do so, but his reservations speak volumes about the nature of cool. Washington's argument was that, since his was a short-lived family, there was a good chance that he might die in office, and it was Washington's one simple desire to be *seen relinquishing power*, that he might be the first American to be *seen stepping down from office*. He was ultimately seen doing so, and the world is better for it. Washington is greater for having done it, because giving away power is the essence of cool. You can always go get more power if you want to, and no one's life is worse for giving it away.

So, critical fashions aside, the issue at the heart of the schism between cool and irony is the question of how art might best serve the ends of democracy. Does it do so by presuming repression and adopting the noisy, servile ironies that must ultimately make it so, or does the work of art simply behave in a democratic manner, presenting itself to us as a cool, powerful embodiment of these values? Does it treat us as fellow slaves or as fellow citizens? I prefer the latter and remain beguiled by the possibility that the generous equanimity and visible integrity of cool objects might, by their very presence, reduce the clamor, create a democracy and promote the idea that the truth need only be seen or spoken and never spoken for.

On the Road Forever

ON THE ROAD narrates the travels of its author, Jack Kerouac (called Sal Paradise in the book), his friend Neal Cassady (called Dean Moriarty in the book), and their friends as they bounce around the North American continent in the late 1940s, like a twelve-rail snooker shot. Sal is the drifter and dreamer; Moriarty is the hustler and jailhouse aristocrat, and neither character demonstrates much in the way of goal-oriented behavior beyond hipster enthusiasm in the quest for fun, girls, adventure, beatitude, and eating that old white line down the highway. Kerouac transforms the narrative of their travels into the last, great hymn to America as a giant landscape you can taste on your tongue, an expanse that means something magical and tolerates whatever the heart can imagine. It is also the longest book ever written in a rush of unrelenting kindness, without a trace of malice. Over the years, Kerouac has served up his America, as if on a platter, to thousands upon thousands of young Americans, myself among them. He has sent them out into the drift and into the night with enough generosity to keep them fairly safe.

This year, 2007, marks the fiftieth anniversary of *On the Road*'s first publication. This means I read it for the first time fifty years ago, when I was in my early teens. I bought the book off the rack, in hardcover, because we were a transient family and the title, *On the Road*, seemed to promise some insight into that peculiar gift and affliction. I remember every detail of my reading the book: the upstairs bedroom of my grandparents' house in south Fort Worth, the dusty scuffs that the black-cloth cover of the book acquired in the process of my reading it; the weave of the tumbled sheets on which I wrestled with Kerouac's language, the shadows cast by my reading lamp on the flowered wallpaper, and the creak of my footsteps on the chilly hardwood floor as I walked from the bed where I was reading to the bathroom where I continued to read.

The book didn't change my life, thank God. It did something better. It confirmed my life as it was. It made me feel breathless and weightless, as if the world were expanding and I was being blown through it like a bubble. It made my own world make a kind of sense, and bestowed on my restless parents a kind of hipster nobility—so I did not read the book again for more than fifteen years. I was afraid that it would not live up to itself. Other authors, Jean-Paul Sartre, Hermann Hesse, and Rainer Maria Rilke, had let me down on rereading. They made me feel like an idiot for my original enthusiasm, so I held off on *On the Road*. When I did read it again, in my early thirties, I was ten years into my life as a professional writer myself, and it was like being hit by a truck.

It was so much better than I ever would have imagined that I wanted to cry. Today, I regard *On the Road* as one of those mysterious icons that renew themselves with every reading, like a candle that burns a different color every time you light it, that somehow evokes pure sentiment without becoming too sentimental. Very few books fall into this category, Hemingway maybe, but not much else. On the lighter side, Kerouac's book also has some cultural parallels with the movie *Spinal Tap*, and, perhaps, I am demeaning Kerouac by this comparison, but *Spinal Tap* and *On the Road* get what they set out to get absolutely right.

Spinal Tap is the single work of art in any media that nails the heart of rock and roll for those of us who played it—nails it with so much precision that it's hard to sort your memory of the film from your memory of your life. [I, too, have wandered in the underground labyrinth of the Agora in Cleveland. I, too, have perused astrological charts prepared by girls who are "with the band."] The same may be said of *On the Road*. It rides with you down every road you travel like an aura indistinguishable from fact.

What ties *Spinal Tap* together with *On the Road* most profoundly, however, is that they both get sadder every time you read the book or see the movie. The first experience is pure joy, absolute, stunning recognition. With each subsequent experience the truth gets tougher; there is more rage in the lunacy and outrageousness. The folly of vanity and demented hope becomes more excruciating. The intensity of the transient pleasure burns like a sparkler in your gut. Today, five times through it, *On the Road* is the saddest, most loving, and candid book in the world. So loving and candid that I feel tentative even writing about it. The book meant so much to Kerouac—*was* so much of Kerouac that he hardly wrote a decent word after other people started writing about it. Thankfully, it took six years to get *On the Road* published, and, during these years, Kerouac produced a parade of speed-crazed masterpieces full of lowbrow ecstasy.

During its long life, *On the Road* has had its seasons. In the first ten years of its public vogue, it was a skyrocket that announced the future of everything. In its second decade, it was an "old-school" skyrocket, a Charlie Parker-John Coltrane skyrocket, that was mostly read by musicians in vans and buses out on the midnight highway. For my musician friends, *On the Road* had the aura of an ancestral text, an American Odyssey whose innocence one had to touch to keep the faith. Everyone who did the road read *On the Road*—from Waylon Jennings to Jeff Beck to Stevie Ray Vaughn to Ian Hunter, to Butch Trucks of the Allman

Brothers. Then, around 1980, *On the Road*'s enthusiasts divided into two schools: University litterateurs had come to appreciate "Kerouac's oracular voice," and outlaw homosexuals, like Robert Mapplethorpe and John Rechy, recognized, in the haunted relationship of Sal and Dean, America's first great gay love story, their Anna Karenina. They passed the book around. It lived, and this is how art lives.

About ten years ago, I uncovered a fourth wave. I taught the book in a graduate art-theory seminar, along with Pynchon, Bolano, Gaddis, Robbe-Grillet and Barthelme. All the tough guys hated Kerouac's book. They thought the characters were lazy and self-absorbed. The gay guys hated it too, because the characters were so disorganized and unfocused on their career options. The young women in the class, however, loved it all. I could see the light in their eyes and the promise behind it. They got it, and I was amazed. Here is one of the major "boy books" in the history of American literature, and these young women were identifying with it, not with its women, who were kind of wussy, but with its tonalities, the tempos, and the ever-receding ephemeral grail.

Somehow, somewhere in the depths of Kerouac's tangled sexuality, he would have been happy about this, I think—happy that he had written a book for all seasons, and all sexes, too. Now, as Auden said of Yeats, Kerouac has become his admirers, and anyone who wants to be a writer, wants to *read* a writer, or just touch the pure gift should read *On the Road* because Kerouac, like Dickens [and almost no one else], can make it float and go. There is a vast difference between works that are written quickly and those that read quickly. Kerouac could do both. He was never as fast at writing as he claimed, but he could drive the words on. He could lift them up off the hard scrabble of the crusty world and let them float like autumn leaves carried along on this little cushion of joy as they hurtled forward. And no matter how sad or horrendous the events being narrated, that cushion of joy is still there, like a clear stream running over pebbles. No story in Dickens or Kerouac is so abject that you do not feel the joy of the author who is writing it. That's writing. The rest is just telling the story, and nobody remembers the story of *On the Road*. They remember the trip.

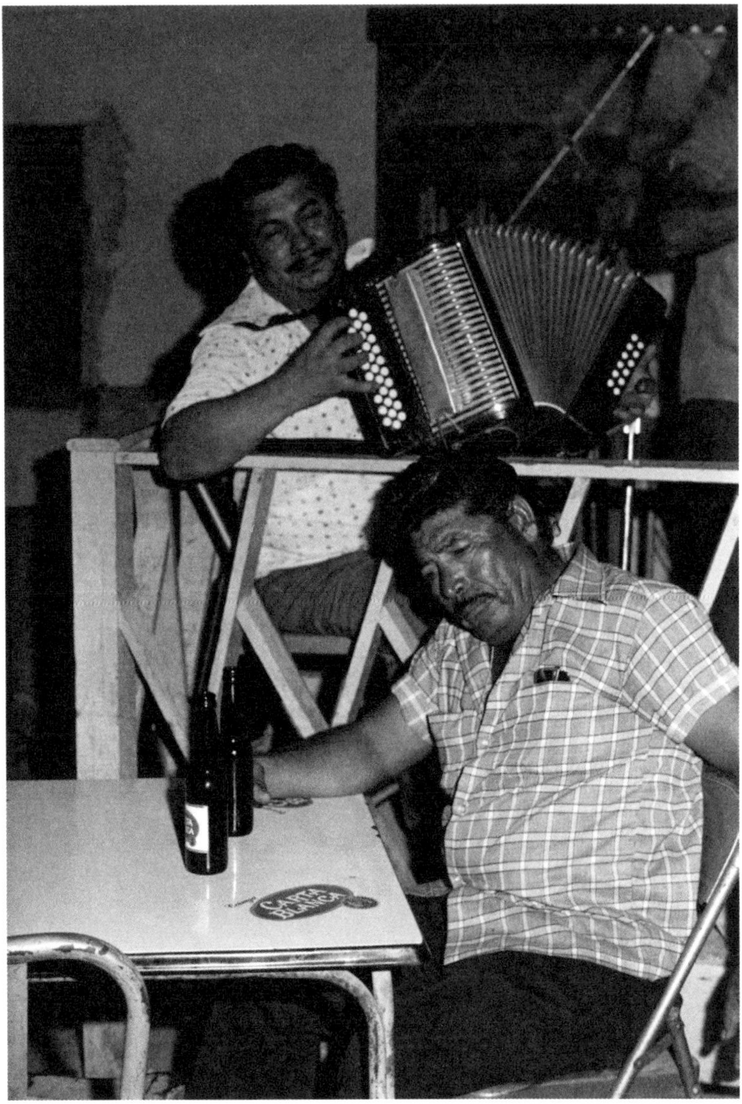

Unidentified photographer
Image from *Boystown*, 1974–75
Silver gelatin print
40.6 × 50.8 cm | 16 × 20 in
Courtesy of The Wittliff Collections, Alkek Library, Texas State University—San Marcos

Nightlife in La Zona

THE photographs collected in *Boystown* are neither historical nor unusual nor particularly rare. In their time and place, they are virtually ubiquitous. Hundreds of thousands of these images were made [and continue to be made] on spec as potential souvenirs by freelance photographers in whorehouses along the border of Texas and Mexico. They document moments in the lives of provincial characters having good, dirty fun, so we could, if we wished, simply dismiss them as trivial images and be done with them as works of art. We could move immediately to the "cultural" and "sociological" implications of the images.

We could do this, but that would occlude the fact that, in our culture, the honorific title of "art" is not intrinsic; it is selected, then selected again and again or, worst-case scenario, *finally selected* in the drift of time. We don't want to forget that Raphael was a skirt-chasing church decorator before we decided that his paintings were "art"—that, before we dubbed Titian's *Venus d'Urbino* [1538] a transcendent masterpiece, it was high-dollar, soft-core pornography whipped up to decorate the bedroom of a provincial bigwig.

Today, the question of what is and what isn't art is subject to a perpetual referendum of preference. Like Roman elections, this referendum is weighted toward the whims of the wealthy, but all images on public view are aspirants to beaux arts status, and anyone who cares about pictures will recognize the whorehouse images in the volume as inheriting a tradition that dates in a steady flow back to the Counter Reformation in seventeenth-century Spain back through Mexico and most of Latin America, where there was no Enlightenment to interrupt the stately progress of the Baroque toward the Romantic and the Modern.

Even the original intentions of the images remain "in style" with this tradition. Before they are anything else, these photographs are ceremonial images. Ceremonial photographers frame their images to mark occasions. The people portrayed in these photographs are conscious of having their picture made and self-consciously pose in attitudes that they consider appropriate to the occasion. Bill Wittliff, the editor of *Boystown*, collected these images and selected the ones he likes, and we will select the images that touch us somehow, with this caveat: since a whorehouse in a border town is the very definition of cultural relativity, the notion of "appropriate pose" varies wildly from sitter to sitter.

The middle-aged *Mexicanos*, in their straw hats, white shirts and khakis, pose themselves with a stiff formality that recalls the society pages of now-defunct cosmopolitan newspapers. The younger *'chucos* hunch forward addressing the camera with tabloid scowls that almost demand booking numbers across their chests; the narco jefes are what they are: expressionless psychopaths; the gangs of *Tejano* fraternity boys happily pose as desperadoes, arranging themselves in tableaux of insolent camaraderie that they have learned from sepia-toned images of the James-Younger Gang or the James boys or Pancho Villa's crew. The girls are adrift. They love the camera and hate their outfits.

The ceremonial occasion of each photograph, then, is local to its individual subject. Each is invariably compromised by the objectivity of the camera's eye. Internal occasions like this are better subjects for the painter's brush, which interprets the light. The angry bang of a flashbulb exploding in a cinder-block structure on a dirt street in a tough town in the great Sonoran desert doesn't give us that ambience of French cosmopolitan gaiety, only the plangent yearning for it. Everywhere [as befits their border setting] these photographs enact the drama of cross-cultural longing.

The middle-aged *Mexicanos* dress like bourgeois Anglo cattlemen; the kids impersonate Chicano gangbangers; the *Tejanos* disguise themselves as Mexican banditos; the young women, caught in the cultural rip tide, are trapped simultaneously in the gaze of the customer and the gaze of the camera. They behave like actresses playing parts in two distinct dramas. In the *mise-en-scène* of the whorehouse, these young women are commodities, objects of sexual desire. The eye of the camera, however, opens on to another world, a world of image, publicity, and sophistication. For them, the tiny portal of the camera's aperture is a *way out* of the circumstances in which they find themselves, so they lift their chins and gaze unsmiling into the camera as fashion models do in slick Anglo magazines, while their bodies, forced into cheap dresses, gleam and bulge like tight, bright sausages and speak the Fellini-esque argot of Mediterranean voluptuousness.

This flirtation with the grotesque distinguishes these photographs from the French pictorial tradition that portrays *la vie bohème* as a glamorous alternative to bourgeois existence. The whorehouse photographs can't disguise the tawdry ephemerality of the setting, the cheap paneling and naked lightbulbs, the mismatched furniture and lumber windows, the rayon draperies, and the sheen of sweat that betrays the pose of insouciance. The camera affirms what the subject seeks to deny, and when an image shows us things that its human subjects dare not see, we enter the older, colder tradition of *vanitas* pictures initiated by

Caravaggio, Velázquez, Sánchez-Cotán, and Murillo.

Vanitas paintings were purportedly dedicated to exposing ephemeral, earthly pleasures and desires. They portrayed people smoking, drinking, eating, singing, dancing, reading, flirting, and gambling. The still lifes portrayed the accoutrements of such activities, the food, pipes, lutes, cards, salmon, dice, and books arranged with skulls, clocks, shadows, and curling smoke—all icons of mutability. The idea was to oppose the eternal Christian values of art to the cheap pleasures of the fleeting moment. The artists, however, outstripped their mandate with virtuoso renderings of the palpable world and ended up communicating a glamorous explosion of surface, color, and detail against which the orders of eternity seem pallid and unrewarding.

This unwitting redemption of the moment is also the benison of these fugitive whorehouse photographs. They are *vanitas* pictures of the first order. They document the failed, illusory poses and personal fantasies of whores and johns balanced on the double-edged blade of nowhere, yet their ultimate effect is far from abject. Maybe this is because I have been there, but what I take away from the photographs is not the folly of such illusions but their necessity in a fallen world—of working stiffs aspiring to the role of *patrons*, of fraternity boys pretending to be outlaws, and whores affecting the cool, affectless gaze of supermodels. The finest photograph in this selection speaks eloquently to this subject. I call it *The Accordian Player*, as Velázquez would have. Its content and composition could have been painted just as easily in 1605 as photographed in the early 1970s.

This image is one of the few "unposed" images in the collection. The photographer "found" this image in the frame of his viewfinder, and this speaks to the strength and liveliness of the Latin Baroque. In the picture's foreground, a middle-aged *borracho* slumps at a table with a bottle in his hand. Another bottle sits on the table beside him. The angle of the photograph tilts the table up as it would be tilted in a seventeenth-century *vanitas*. Above and behind the drinker, elevated on a low stage behind a latticed rail, an accordion player leans forward serenading him. The rectangles of the room, the angles of the lattice, the fan of the accordion, and the two human bodies arrange themselves into a long slow curve that organizes the image and perfectly conforms to the conventions of the genre.

The visible exhaustion and inebriation of the drinker and the self-absorption of the accordionist are perfectly "in style" as well. They tell us what Velázquez would tell us: that life is hard, existence is tawdry, and human beings are foolish and corrupt, but there is still some spark of heart and generosity in the rituals of respite, some comfort in having a clean, well lighted place to go and people to be with, even at the cruel, exploitative edges of human civilization. The lesson of the photograph itself, however, is not that things haven't changed in three centuries. Twentieth-century Mexico is not seventeenth-century Seville. What doesn't change, or changes very little, is muscle memory and the habits of the eye that survive in the chronological memory.

No images come bereft of secular agendas. No images come totally unredeemed by the prompt book of global art and cinema. In photography, particularly, the voyeur's clammy remoteness and the fetishist's pathological romance are integral to process. No photograph presents itself unsullied by revulsion or desire. Even so, the content is always knowable, and all these pictures are dirty with frozen time. They freeze snippets of the life lived before the death of those portrayed in the blink of the shutter. Nothing embodies the chilly specificity of the instant with more poignancy or authority.

Since death is the occluded subject of all photographs, the contemplation of loss and death is never totally absent from our viewing of them. Thus, the whorehouse pictures in *Boystown*, simply because they are photographs, imprint timeless instants, because the language of memory does not survive collected in libraries and museums. It *lives* in our eyes as a reflexive repertoire of options through which we might redeem the fleeting tawdriness of the present in redemptive memory and somehow rescue our foolish fantasies of dignity, power, and nobility from their obvious incongruity. They tease a spark of courage and generosity from our perpetual self-delusion.

Nurturing Your Addictions

IT SEEMS reasonable to assume that the percentage of human beings with the talent and predisposition to make good art and literature has not varied much since the Middle Ages. The equipment and opportunities to make good art and literature, however, has expanded in every decade since the death of John Keats. Elite cultures have responded to this broadening franchise. They defend their domain and status by escalating the level of "difficulty" demanded from serious art and literature. The larger the field of runners on the track, it would seem, the higher the hurdles they must clear. Two centuries of expanding opportunities and an escalating standard of difficulty have led to this consequence: Today, anybody can make a work of art that nobody can understand. Actually, if you factor in the contemporary fantasy that certain kinds of understanding are culturally exclusive, you have a situation in which anybody can make a work of art that nobody has the *right* to understand.

So we live in a moment when works of art are defined by their opacity. We don't care what they mean, so shut up Mr. Critic. The art criticism and commentary that once sought to endow difficult works of art with an element of appreciation and transparency is now regarded with suspicion. Members of the art world, like the adepts of a mystery cult, tread softly, lest some casual explanation shatter the altars at which they worship, so it's no wonder that they are protective of their ignorance. The hegemony of such willful incuriosity seems an appropriate occasion to sort out the costs and benefits of graduate education in art in the United States, the sites in which the franchise is extended and the regime of difficulty is escalated. On these sites, educators with marginal credentials indoctrinate students of marginal literacy in a discourse that is utterly irrelevant. The wind shear cuts hard in these environments and nothing moves.

So let me begin my mild screed against art education by admitting I that spent ten great years teaching graduate students in art in Las Vegas, Nevada. All I did consciously was abolish group crits, admit graduate students from good schools in big cities, and insist that I was there to help, but if you're not sick, don't call the doctor. I had one class with seven real artists in it, all of whom now have careers. My students who were not artists, unfortunately, derived no benefit from my classes. My colleagues talked to me about "raising consciousness," increasing "self-awareness," and encouraging "critical thinking." My resistance to these sociological options ultimately cost me my job, but it was fun while it lasted. Second positive caveat: the American art world as it exists today is founded on one of the great educational experiments in the history of civilization—the GI Bill, which allowed veterans of the armed services to study art with whom they wished wherever they wished—at the Sorbonne in Paris, at Ruskin School of Drawing and Fine Art at Oxford, at the American Academy in Rome, in Kansas City, Chicago, or New York. Ellsworth Kelly, Richard Diebenkorn, Kenneth Noland, Robert Rauschenberg, Leon Golub, Philip Pearlstein, Norman Bluhm, Romare Bearden, Robert Colescott, Larry Rivers, Al Leslie, Sam Francis, and Robert Indiana were beneficiaries of this bill—a pretty good start on an art world that wouldn't have nearly enough women for twenty years.

The expiration and rewriting of the GI Bill and the wave of American exceptionalism that followed in the wake of New York School painting destroyed the cosmopolitan dimension of American art education. It retreated to American universities with adjacent livestock and very little adjacent art. Three kinds of graduate schools evolved from this retrenchment. There were "normal" schools that recruited graduate students as teaching assistants to do the faculty's work for them. Students at these schools, one hopes, learned enough about academia to avoid it henceforth. There were "feeder" schools in New York and Los Angeles that dwelt in the tyrannical shadow of the marketplace. Students from these schools occasionally succeeded by fortuitous shortsightedness. Then there are "seminaries" where students are indoctrinated into last year's intellectual fashion. These schools take students and rob them of their birthright.

Throughout my tenure in the art world, these distinctions have held true—as has the ninety-eight percent rate of attrition among graduates with Masters of Fine Arts degrees. Potential graduates must choose between the wan protocols of academic culture in the provinces, the high-dollar frenzy of the marketplace, or carrying forth the theological rigor of some pale guru. None of these cruel adaptations have much to do with making art, and they all exact a price. Until the late 1970s, no one worried much about this. There were not many graduate students. There were not that many graduate schools. The schools didn't cost that much or pay that much. Artistic poverty was still in fashion, so those who chose the safer path of teaching were seen to deserve their fate. Professors accepted the damage as part of the cost of doing business. Lives were ruined, of course, and hearts were broken. Students were lied to, abused, and deceived. Unlicensed psychotherapy stifled blithe spirits, but this seemed an acceptable price to pay to thin the turkey herd.

In the early 80s, great teachers like John Baldessari at CalArts and Michael Craig-Martin at Goldsmiths gave graduate education some career credibility. Soon thereafter, art schools were mandated to enhance their liberal arts credentials. Most schools embraced the culture-theory-diversity business. Most tried to imbue art practice with liberal arts disciplines. None, however, tried to imbue the liberal arts with the louche permissions of the artist's studio. Many art departments transformed themselves into boot camps for theoretical regimes that had their own generalissimos. These stars justified an exponential increase in the cost of graduate education. They attracted a ballooning number art-graduate students who hoped that smart made art. The rate of attrition, however, stayed steady. There was no Golden Age, no cornucopia of new art, no legions of new artists. Graduate art students were reduced to bagmen. They borrowed a quarter-million bucks from the government, gave it to the university to build the dean a house, and then worked in an Apple store to pay the bill. This is best described as a win-win-lose proposition.

Even serious graduate educators in cultural practice, sadly, can only strive to do no harm. They cannot create artists, and, should one appear, the window of opportunity they once flung open is now closed by established doctrine. I offer this example: In 1992, I was given a tour of the architectural drawing studio at Cornell University—a long stone shed with a long line of drafting tables facing a long line of windows looking out onto the weeds and snow puddles of bucolic Ithaca. As we walked in, the common boom box was booming Jane's Addiction. Perry Farrell was yelping his way through "Mountain Song," "Summertime Rolls," and other frenzied chestnuts. I raised an eyebrow at my professorial minder. He declined to acknowledge the music, refused, even, to raise his voice to be heard over it.

We walked behind the long row of students hunched over their boards lining out pale, pure modern architecture, straight up, no olive, no onion, no twist. I imagined a red fireman's axe embedded in each student's skull, the axe handles running down their backs, the blades splitting each student brain left from right. Right brain: Jane's Addiction and feckless ecstasy. Left brain: Colin Rowe and impotent modernism. In the fleeting moment after I heard the music and before I saw the drawings, I had experienced an uptick of interest. Architecture infused with Jane's Addiction might be fun, and it might have been. I mentioned this schism to my academic minder once we were outside. "Oh yes," he murmured, "We like to wipe the slate clean here."

I wondered how many slate-wipings were required to disable the bicameral mind altogether, but I didn't ask for fear the requisite number would be immediately forthcoming. Then, as I always do, I tried to imagine the fate of my ideal student under such a regimen. The graduate student of my professorial dreams would be the Quentina Tarantino of American art. She would bring with her the same knowledgeable enthusiasm for postwar art that Tarantino brings for postwar cinema. She would want to do art from jump, and I can't imagine a school in the world where she would flourish. Depending on the school, she would be labeled as disruptive, arrogant, or unteachable, and, trust me, she would be. I know this because even my second most-ideal students had trouble. The kids who brought keyboards, piles of books, comic books, mascara, starburst clocks, Fiesta ware, firecrackers, golf clubs, surfboards, and sexy underwear all suffered for their stake in the living culture.

Then I tried to imagine famous slates wiped clean. I imagined Andy Warhol's slate wiped clean of all that advertising crap, Richard Serra denied his greasy shipyard, Matthew Barney denied his preppy, jock dandyism, Jim Rosenquist denied his billboard skills, Barbara Kruger sans *Mademoiselle*, Laurie Anderson and Mike Kelley without rock and roll, Tom Nozkowski without *Mad* magazine, Jim Shaw without Freddy Krueger, Lari

Pittman without the poof and glitter of the decorator shop. All of these situations are unimaginable, and this has made twenty years of watching similar atrocities visited upon graduate students all the sadder. Some will say that these students just weren't tough enough, even though young artists shouldn't *need* the ability to recognize aggression in the guise of care; it shouldn't be required as part of an artist's skill set. Now it is.

My optimum solution would be to abolish graduate studies in art altogether. Failing this, one might just avoid it. Try the late Michael Balog's solution: make surfboards that are better than art then make art like that. Try Raymond Pettibon's trajectory: grow up in a literary family in a beach house full of books, get a degree in economics, teach math, draw posters for your brother's band [Black Flag], hang out, and get discovered. Or Josiah McElheny's trajectory: study anthropology, become interested in single-source traditions like glassblowing, go to Italy and study that tradition, learn to blow glass from the masters, and start making art. Or, as a last resort, try the solution my classmate Gilbert Shelton fell upon. Gilbert and his crew went up to the art department at the University of Texas every day and painted Abstract Expressionism. Every night, they came home to draw posters and underground comic books. When they had enough pages, they founded Zap Comix and moved to San Francisco. Finally, they moved to Paris, where they still draw comics.

All these strategies seem riskier and more circuitous than graduate school, but they work better and don't hurt nearly as much. They don't include cinderblock walls. There are no creepy has-beens with sour admonitions or nincompoops in the food court. No would-be househusband would try to teach you to create 1979 Datsuns, just like he did in 1979. More to the point, in the egg-and-spoon race for artistic recognition, you are a thousand times more likely to get there with your egg if you avoid graduate school. More critically, if you want to be an artist and you *must* go to graduate school, *you must bring your own egg*, your junk, your talisman, your jones, your touchstone in the larger culture. It has to be something that you love, even if it's just an old Hobie or a street tag or Jane's Addiction. You need something whose loss you are sure to notice if it begins to slip away, something to serve as a hedge against ignorant opacity, because it's not just about you, kid, it's about bringing the fire from wherever you found it to an art world that desperately needs it.

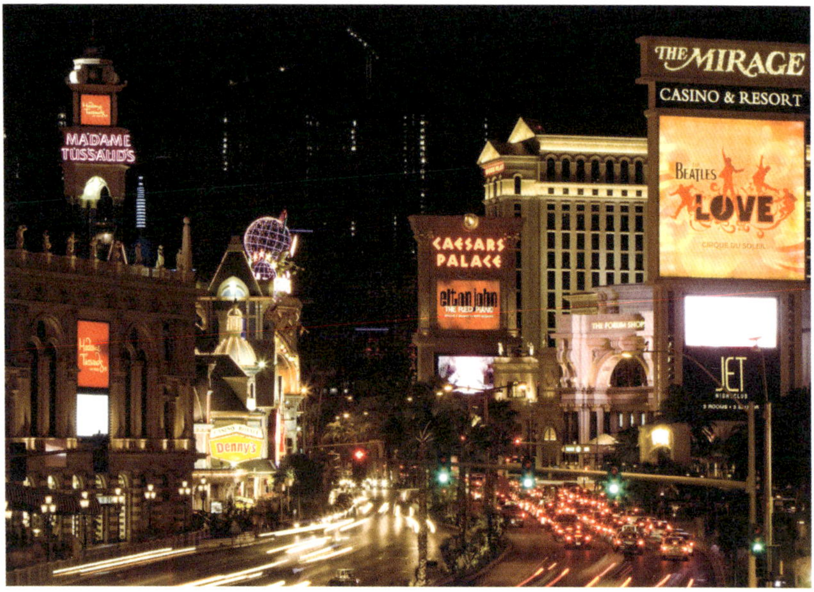

The Las Vegas Strip, 2009

Las Vegas for Sissies

WHAT can I tell serious art people about Las Vegas? Just this: You should not worry about it. Vegas is a nice town—bland as a biscuit in the sunshine, pastel and haunted in the morning and in the evening when the glow of the sky matches the glow of the neon. Under the stars, it is the absolute, incarnate, dazzled heart of earthly promise. You can gamble here, of course, and glamour is not illegal, nor is the night, but otherwise the ordinary laws and customs of cosmopolitan society are genially in place and tolerantly enforced. As a consequence, only Mecca has more visitors every year. I lived there for twenty years and even though fifteen years is too long to live anywhere, I think of Vegas as my home, because I genuinely like it; I like the weather, the palm trees, the crap-tables, the showrooms, the music, the bars [cocktail and titty], the restaurants, the fountains, the airport, the hours, the people, the pace, and, most of all, I like the lights. I like nearly everything, in fact, except the traffic and the unctuous air of social concern exuding from the junketing culturati whom I encounter on a regular basis.

In academia, I am the "Vegas guy," and during the past twelve months, I have spoken with forty journalists, minimum, in Vegas on assignment from icy climes—journalists from New York,

Auckland, Prague, Stockholm, Frankfurt, Montreal, London, Minneapolis, etc. They all insist that they have come because they are "interested" in Las Vegas, but they are not. They are *worried* about Las Vegas. During the same period, I spoke with easily a hundred "serious" architects, recently flown in from climates comparably frigid. They claim to be "interested" in Las Vegas, too. They are not either. They are even more worried than the journalists, and I don't understand this. I am not worried about Auckland or Cambridge, so why are they worried about Las Vegas? Are people being *trained* to worry about Vegas at the Fun Police Academy, or what—or maybe Vegas-worry is a self-selecting vocation? It's a mystery, for sure, but lately I've been thinking that maybe it has something to do with the millennium, because, earthly virtues aside, Vegas does have its eschatological moments.

I remember a blue, summer evening about a week after my wife and I came to town. We were cruising down the Strip listening to Pink Floyd on the car radio when, *kaboom!*, this operatic desert thunderstorm exploded all around us. The rain crashed down in sheets, engulfing everything. Light from the setting sun continued to banner in over the mountains, spangling through the plunging water. The Strip seethed and sizzled around us like a neon flash fire, its colors bleeding on the windshield. Mile-high lightning trees crackled down the blue-black curve of the southern sky, and then, as if to summon the dead, this heart-stopping clap of thunder magically synchronized with the opening chords of "Another Brick in The Wall (Part III)" on the car radio. That was pretty apocalyptic and pretty exciting, too, but I didn't get *worried* about it. All I thought was, "Home at last!"

But that's just me. Other cultural speculators who have not come to Vegas to gamble, dine, drink, dance, and smoke, who do not dream of wandering through the rose-colored dawn with a roll of hundreds in their shirt pocket, a bimbo on their arm, and a cocktail in their hand, just don't get it. These dudes have documentary projects, research grants, and magazine assignments. That's what they tell you, although I am virtually certain that each of them fears that this is not the *real* reason for their pilgrimage. They are fearful of being lured into the neon cauldron by some deeper and possibly fatal attraction, as Gladstone was drawn to the whores. They step onto the Strip as Gladstone stepped into brothels—hysterically *en garde*. They will not gamble and they will not tip, because gambling and tipping are voluntary and, after that first act of volition, well, you know: *Le déluge*! Soon they become annoyed that not gambling and not tipping is *their* responsibility—that they *could* be gambling, and they *should* be tipping, and they would be tipping and gambling but even this flicker of temptation initiates worry about their money. They imagine it flying away, evaporating, but this embarrasses them, so they start worrying about *other people*'s money—the money of those less *en garde* who are good-naturedly gambling and tipping all around them. They envision all humankind betting on a tumbling die, as, of course, they do. *Then*, they start worrying about Las Vegas.

Twenty minutes afterward, I meet them for a drink, but the payoff comes later in the evening. We are standing around over at the Hard Rock as a Nine Inch Nails concert is letting out, or a Ray Charles concert, or an Eric Burdon concert, even. People stream around us in noisy bunches, laughing, lighting cigarettes, and sloshing drinks. Wired and fairly bouncing, they wade out on to the casino floor like a boarding party of pirates, yanking out their wallets and ready to win a fucking bazillion at the tables. When the surge of the crowd has passed us, dispersing into the *fête*, my visiting scribe from the North looks solemnly over at me, seeking eye contact. When I look back, he shakes his head wistfully and, almost on the verge of tears, says: "It's a kind of *despair*, isn't it, Dave?" I just say no and suggest this place that has great calamari at two in the morning.

Visiting architects, I should note, are desperate creatures anyway, so they do not harp on despair. They wring their hands like my great aunt Florence and exclaim, "It's so distracting! It's so distracting!" They always say this twice for some reason, and I always say, "From what?" although I know: Vegas distracts them from the comfortable, narcissistic state of inner contemplation that is the human spirit's last refuge from the arctic deprivations of "serious architecture"—but, what the hell, that's okay too. Certainly, it's preferable to the visiting art student from Berlin who actually burst into tears as the Dunes exploded in front of her, crying out plaintively that she was in Hell! Hell! [Saying things twice as an intensive, I should note, is an interesting contemporary idiosyncrasy.] So here's what I have in mind: Since I take no pleasure in the distress and worry visited upon fellow members of the cultural community who visit *mi barrio*, I have prepared some observations and suggestions that may save you worry and, possibly, a trip.

First, be assured that you do not have to gamble to have fun in Las Vegas. We *do* have whores, but you really should tip. If, however, you are not, in some sense, a gambler, if you take no pleasure in risking something of value on the chance of something more valuable still, Vegas will be totally opaque to you, so you should probably stay home. Vegas is a gambling town. That's all it is, from edge to edge and top to bottom. Its rules are gambling-town rules. I share these with you as they were enumerated for me by Dr. Herb "Speedy" Newman, a retired dope smuggler and "sports investor" with whom I breakfast occasionally at the Bagelmania Deli down on Twain. Speedy was eighty-one last month. They took away his pilot's license ten years ago but he is still bright as a minnow, sharp enough to make a living betting hoops, and he loves Las Vegas.

"And Vegas," he told me years ago, "got just three rules: *No Sissies. No Dummies. Full Accountability*. You got to have *cojones* to wager; you got to have the brains to bet right, and you got to have the honor to pay off when you lose." (This would explain why Nevada is among the least educated states in the country with the highest per capita IQ.) Speedy, of course refrains from mentioning the unspoken rule—the one that underpins his practical axioms. He doesn't mention it because one refrains from mentioning the name of God, but it accounts for his lightness and brightness at eighty-one. That rule is simply this: You have to be an optimist; you have to believe that you can handicap the future—because the future is *always* what you're betting on. You calculate the odds, take the chance and pay your debts. Gambling is an optimist's vocation, and tomorrow is always out there with a brand-new shuffle in the filigree of statistical alternatives.

That's why I live in Las Vegas. After languishing for thirty years in the cultural ghetto, breathing its miasma of fashionable pessimism, absorbing its rhetoric of inevitable decline, moral helplessness, trust-fund babies, and ineluctable historical logic, I just wanted to hang out where people actually *did* things on their own dime, right or wrong, brave or foolish. So here is my best advice: if you don't like the action, go to Boston. Don't come out here to Vegas and whine to me about global warming, existential despair, creeping totalitarianism, and proliferating late capitalism. I see the same world you do, so if you want to swim in this pond, take your measure, quote me some odds, pull out your bankroll, and let's fucking *bet*. I may lose, but if we're all still here tomorrow, we can bet again. That will be exciting.

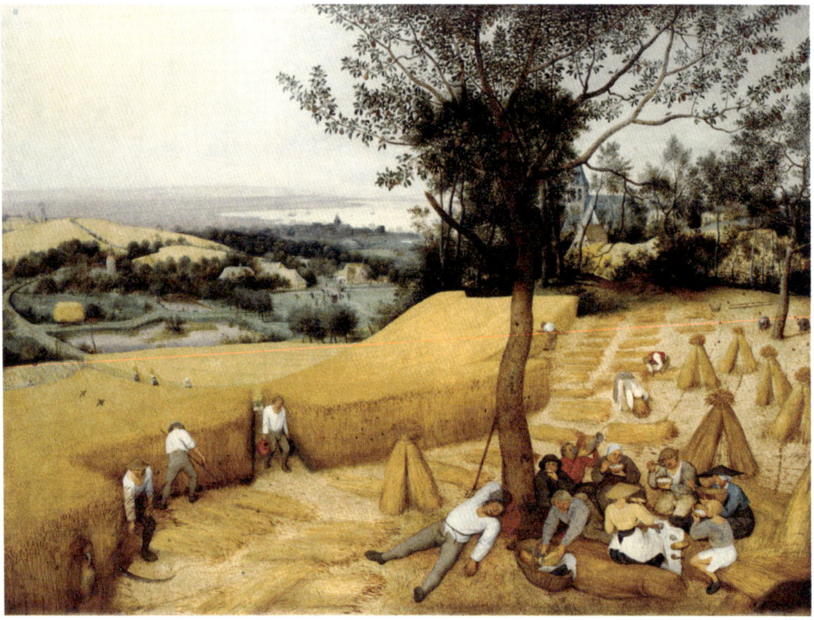

Pieter Bruegel the Elder
The Harvesters, 1565
Oil on wood
119 × 162 cm | 46⅞ × 63¾ in

Backstory

IN 1565, Pieter Bruegel the Elder painted *The Harvesters* in Antwerp for his friend and patron Niclaes Jongelinck. During the next few years, Antwerp was ransacked and burned twice—first by the Spanish and then by the French—but *The Harvesters* survived. In 1594, the painting was in the hands of Hane von Wijke, who sold Bruegel's work for 1,400 florins to the Antwerp City Council. They gave it to Archduke Ernst, the new governor of the Netherlands. The archduke took *The Harvesters* to Brussels and into the sphere of the Hapsburgs. As a result, when Ernst died in 1595, the Holy Roman Emperor Rudolf II plucked up *The Harvesters* and had it delivered to Prague.

Rudolf was a special collector, even for an emperor. He was a linguist, astrologer, alchemist, and more than half mad—this last being a trait that courtiers tend to overlook in their emperors. So they overlooked it while Rudolf built a collection of paintings, sculptures, decorative objects, instruments, machines, books, precious stones, rocks, plants, birds, and animals. He had nearly bankrupted the empire by the time they led him off to count the butterflies. At his death in 1612, Rudolf's collection was largely dispersed, but not Bruegel's painting, which the Hapsburgs considered to be among their jewels.

The Harvesters was kept in the family and moved to the new imperial residence in Vienna, where it became the property of Archduke Leopold Wilhelm, a tougher, smarter and more ruthless collector than Rudolf. When Leopold Wilhelm moved to Brussels as governor of the Netherlands, he hired the painter David Teniers as his curator and set about collecting big time. When Leopold Wilhelm died in 1662, his paintings were moved back to Vienna and into the care of Emperor Leopold I, who preferred music to art. When Leopold I died in 1705, *The Harvesters* became part of the larger imperial collection.

Eventually, centuries of religious wars and revolutions began to take their toll. Hapsburg treasures slipped away. Courtiers made off with paintings. Storehouses were pillaged. A great gathering of Northern European paintings was looted, carted off to Sweden, and destroyed in a fire. The bulk of the imperial collection, containing many Bruegels, would become the pride of Vienna's Kunsthistorisches Museum in 1891, but in 1809 *The Harvesters* turned up in Paris in the possession of Comte Antoine-François Andréossy, an Austrian soldier who had distinguished himself as one of Napoleon's artillery officers. Andréossy auctioned *The Harvesters* in 1816 for not too many francs, because the glamour of the Hapsburgs was fading. The appeal of sturdy peasants was declining, and Bruegel's reputation had never been strong in France.

The next known possessor of *The Harvesters* was Jacques Antoine Doucet, a fashionable Parisian painter, dilettante, and connoisseur. Around 1912, Doucet sold the painting to Paul Jean Cels, a collector of Flemish art in Brussels whose health was subsequently ravaged in the trenches. In 1919, following World War I, Cels sold *The Harvesters* to the Metropolitan Museum of Art in New York. He used the money to emigrate to Australia. Once there, Cels sold the rest of his Flemish paintings at bargain prices to the National Gallery of Australia in Canberra, where he could see his paintings cared for properly. Fortunately,

Cels left *The Harvesters* to me.

In the mid-1950s, after my freshman year as a math and engineering student at Southern Methodist University, I continued my summer pilgrimages to Manhattan. Usually I went by bus and read Henry Miller in the window seat. Once I hitchhiked. Once I got a ride as far as New Orleans and didn't escape the Big Easy until September. Once I rode with a friend in a stolen Buick. Once I had the loan of an apartment in New York. For a few years, I had a girlfriend who danced in Broadway choruses. Early on, though, I slept on the couches of friends whose girlfriends were happier when I didn't hang around all day. So Manhattan became my playground once I found places to pee and to play.

I was sixteen when these pilgrimages began. I don't know why they did or why I chose Manhattan. For a teenager, I was not that unhappy, but I had been on my own for years, so I tended to proceed without much planning or introspection, just to see what I would do. What I did when I got to Manhattan was acquire a student card from the New York Public Library and a summer pass to the Met and the Cloisters. These places were all cheap and strategically located, and you could pee there without encountering too many unwelcome erotic opportunities. You could also spend whole days exploring them. Eventually I discovered the Frick, and a lot of Midtown art galleries where they would let you use the toilet. Conrad and Carroll Janis would also pull paintings from the storage racks to show me. They were so kind that I cringe today imagining what being sixteen and just off the bus from Texas must have looked like to them.

Whenever possible, I ate lunch at the Museum of Modern Art because you could meet girls there, ideally tall dancers with Ace bandages around their ankles who wore Bengay like perfume. The rest of the time I looked at paintings, went to movies and attended plays (lots of Jean Genet in the Village). Then I went to the library to read about them in the press and the journals. The museums and galleries were best because they were always empty. In the middle of this mighty, crowded, noisy city, I could stroll like a prince through my own salons, examining my treasures: first among them *The Harvesters*. I religiously visited the painting and developed an acquaintance with a guard named Chaim who had been standing contentedly in that room for two decades. Chaim knew all there was to know about Flemish painting.

I was particularly beguiled by *The Harvesters*, because I hate Northern European painting generally. I hate itty-bitty jewel-like realism and *really* hate depictions of sturdy peasants in the agribusiness. I got enough of that in Texas so I was Huysmans's Des Esseintes, *a rebours*, against nature and against the grain. At the New York Public Library, I found that scholars wanted to know if *The Harvesters* is one of four paintings (representing the seasons), or one of twelve (one per month). I wanted to know why I liked a painting whose subject matter I found tedious, and which I couldn't imagine the Hapsburgs liking any better than I did. And how did it get here?—this 400-year-old *thing* borne forth through the centuries by human beings, institutions, and governments that had burned to ash, or crumbled into dust, and left it behind.

For an adolescent and a nonprofessional, this was an exciting concept, so I skipped lunch one day and used my money to buy a print of *The Harvesters* from the Met's bookshop. I took it home and spread it out on my friends' dining table in the dark of night. I borrowed their yardstick, and—like the good little engineer I was, and like the eighteenth-century philosopher I wasn't—I followed my instincts by lamplight and figured the damn thing out. Here is the short version. The proportion of the panel is two to three. Two overlapping squares divide the width of the painting into vertical thirds. A tree marks as the right side of the left-hand square. The innermost harvester working at the wheat marks the left edge of the right-hand square. The left third of the painting contains three working harvesters. The center third contains one sleeping harvester. The right third contains eight harvesters relaxing, and there is probably a good rationale for the numbered groups.

A yellow peak of standing wheat marks the center of the painting from whence an Italian virgin has been evicted. A double "S" curve twines like ivy around the diagonal line rising from the lower-left corner to the upper right—beginning on the lower left as a curve of standing wheat and ending at the upper right as a curve of sky revealed through tree branches. This made me feel funny, because the design I had conjured up was rational enough to be deliberate. And if it was deliberate, Occam's razor suggested that it was too elegant to be my own idea or Bruegel's; it was obviously a well-executed, traditional maneuver, like the pick-and-roll in basketball. This meant that, for 400 years, everyone who had looked at *The Harvesters* had been looking at the same musculature beneath the skin of paint. This musculature had to be a factor in the painting's survival—because it was always there, however you read the painting's story.

The next day I rolled up my diagram and took it to the Met. They wouldn't let me bring it in, so I went up and explained it to Chaim. He said I was right, and how did he know I was right? I didn't know, so he told me about the thin strips of wood that had been added to the top, bottom, and right edges of the panel. These strips meant one of three things. Maybe Bruegel began laying out the painting, noticed the proportions were wrong and changed them. Or, maybe Bruegel brought the panel into proportion before he started. Or, maybe someone—maybe Bruegel—fixed the proportions after the fact. In all cases, the strips and my armature confirmed one another. Wow.

Today, I don't like *The Harvesters* that much, but the payoff of liking the painting then was so enormous that it still shocks me. I grew up in Fort Worth, Texas, a city of paintings, and I quickly became an adept of provenance and design before I was ever an "art person." I know things now that really help, because I was once young and alone in Manhattan with days to waste in wondering, because I was a whiz at math and design, and purely devoted to my own adolescent enthusiasm. Out of that tangle of faults and misperceptions, I got to sit in the reading room and inhale commercial Antwerp in the sixteenth century and hang with crazy Rudolf II, his great paintings, his crocodiles, chameleons, birds of paradise, pelicans, and turtles.

I got an exotic taste of the giddy, greedy Hapsburgs, a glimpse of a Napoleonic artillery officer who made off with a masterpiece, and a peek at a Parisian *flâneur* who bought Bruegel's painting cheap and sold it high to a Belgian connoisseur who [in effect] sold it to me. Add to this the sheer serendipity of Chaim being there to tell me that I wasn't wrong. So, today, when I wander into the Met, I always imagine the museum in ruins, as it one day will be, like Rudolf's garden, and when this happens, nothing will really change. The wonderful, defenseless things that survive will still be somewhere in the world. Their survival will still depend on the acuity of willful enthusiasts, like Archduke Leopold Wilhelm, Chaim the museum guard, and a footloose teenager from Texas, all of whom had their eyes open.

Art Collectors

MY LIFE has no narrative, but it has had some nice vignettes. About ten years ago, we were all in Steve Wynn's old office on the ground floor of the Mirage Casino and Resort in Las Vegas. It is a large rectangular room with shining Schindler-esque plate-glass walls on three of its sides surrounded by a garden of palms, exotic succulents, and decorative cacti. Libby and I stood against the long glass wall on the north. Libby was Steve's curator. (Julia Roberts plays her in *Ocean's Eleven*, although not to Libby's satisfaction. I mean, those shoes!) I was just there for the art. There was a beautiful mid-size Jackson Pollock hanging in front of the west window. Across from me, Giacometti's life-size *Man Pointing* (1947) was walking and pointing. On the couch beside the Giacometti, the golfer Nancy Lopez was just there for the fun. On a large round table in the center of the office, an exquisite grayish Cézanne portrait of a seated woman was laying faceup. My friend Richard Shiff was bending over Cézanne's canvas examining every inch of its surface with a magnifying glass. Richard is a Cézanne wonk and a top-of-the-line contemporary critic.

Steve sat behind his long desk against the eastern glass wall with his back to the Strip. He talked to all of us individually and as a group, and talked on the phone. He quizzed Libby about the proper frame, asked me about Steve Martin's Roy Lichtenstein and whether he should buy it. [Yes, he should, and keep the frame.] He kept quizzing Richard about the Cézanne. Is it a great one? What would be Richard's ballpark price? What about the blur on the woman's face? Is there any visible damage or restoration? Richard only answered the technical questions, but Steve was moving on, trying to get Bill Clinton on the phone about a golfing date with Nancy Lopez. Libby paid very close attention to the painting's condition. Nancy was enjoying the whole, energetic spectacle. I chatted with Richard about politics at the University of Texas, my alma mater, where Richard is a distinguished professor. I also found myself trying to imagine a collection of more disparate and talented people among greater works of art in a gaudier room anywhere else in the world. We were all experts of one sort or another. It was like a scene from a Mughal palace at the height of the Empire that was founded, appropriately enough, by descendants of Genghis Khan—the Bugsy Siegels of their era. Here we were in Steve's office with all this great art, all these strange people, and there was a fucking *Cézanne*, just lying there on a table!

This was a comfortable place for me because I knew art collectors long before I knew any artists. My parents would drag us to parties, and I hated the tininess and powerlessness of being a child, so I gravitated toward adults who were ecumenically enthusiastic—to horse people, art collectors, and music mavens. They would talk to anyone about what they loved, so I learned about stud fees, Milton Resnick, and Bird Parker. Our social position in south Fort Worth was such that I didn't learn that my family wasn't rich until high school when Scotty's dad bought him a Porsche. I had my own apartment, two paper routes, and a coral and cream Ford Victoria, so this didn't bother me.

My friends loved the oil business. I wanted to be a Walter

Pidgeon professor with a smoking jacket, sherry, and leather-bound books. I didn't learn that universities were a sham until later. I didn't learn that graduate schools were tacky, spiteful dungeons until much later, and I abandoned one for the art business because it seemed cozy and out of sight, sort of like a noir Junior League with fine lingerie and quality drugs. You needed stationery and a business card. You needed a tasteful living room and dining room in which to hang the art, and I am from Fort Worth where people keep things in their houses. We Fort Worth people are all a lot like Wemmick in *Great Expectations*. We do like our portable property.

One of my senior homeys, gesturing toward his Tintoretto, told me, "I like to sit right here in my boots, smoke a cigar, and look at it. I don't like to sit in an auditorium in Dallas that stinks of hair spray watching some Russian jump around in his underwear." As much as I love the dance, I share a lot with my senior homey. I don't much like parties. I am indifferent to social status, except at the baccarat table. I don't even care about the rich unless we're looking at art. Otherwise, hanging with the rich is like standing in a strong wind talking about French duvets.

One night, thirty years ago, I found myself in Acapulco with some Texas collectors, halfway through a spontaneous banquet on a hotel balcony overlooking the Pacific with warm breezes and moonbeams sparkling on the ocean. The evening went on and on. There was singing and laughter. Waiters rushed to the table with more food, more wine, and more cocktails. Across the table from me, a couple were talking about taking the party on to Brussels. I was thinking that, if I had to pay for any of this, I would have to ride home on a Mexican bus. I didn't, but I hated that feeling of floating impotence, and I would rather not have been there. So I am a bad courtier, for which I am happy. Otherwise, had I *wished* to attend any of the hundreds of thousands of similar social occasions to which I have not been invited or declined to attend, I would probably resent art collectors, but I don't. Envy is a scumbag vice.

Also I share many interests with art collectors, and my optimal social situation is sitting in a room with a few people in casual attire, talking about something on the wall. The decorum of communicating through the medium of an object has a quiet, cowboy courtesy about it, like wranglers sitting around a campfire talking into the flames, and it suits me. Also, I love the waft, flutter, and filigree of desire, insight, self-revelation, and sublimation. I love to watch the courage of careful citizens blossom on their walls. I still cherish the first cool rush of the crazy things that I saw in people's houses back in Fort Worth.

Back in that day, I loved Jim Meeker's handsome, mid-century crash pad on the Ridglea golf course—where I met Charlie Watts and Dennis Hopper—where I saw Grace Slick zonked out on the leather couch above which hung Edward Ruscha's *Standard Station, Amarillo, Texas* [1963]. I fell in love twice in about one second. Years later, I met Grace fully conscious, but Jim gave his wonderful Ruscha to the Hood Museum at Dartmouth where, if you stand up close and sniff, you can still get high. At Ed and Ann Hudson's house, I was introduced to a Brice Marden waxwork, a Lynda Benglis pour, a Don Judd woody, a Carl Andre flat, and Andy's silver Liz diptych.

One afternoon, Henry Hopkins and I dropped by Sid Bass's condo. Henry was director of the Modern Art Museum of Fort Worth. I was just tagging along. Sid answered the door with the phone in his hand, six hours into a telephone conversation with Bob Irwin in California. Sid's new Irwin disc was glowing on the wall. Henry and I marveled at the disc. Sid and Bob said their goodbyes, then Sid hung up, and we started all over again. So I was very lucky for a young civilian. That cool waterfall of tiny, pleasant surprises probably saved my life, although I still wonder if coming upon new art unawares, in domestic settings, was a blessing or a curse.

Works of art in museums, as wonderful as they are, always feel naked and bereft to me. They belong to other people, and they all have their homes. I am thankful to see them and covet them, of course, and I like to see collectors' judgment confirmed. The tragedy of rich people, I always tell collectors who seek my advice, is that they can have *anything*, but they can't have *everything*. The world presents itself to them as an infinite array of potentially rotten decisions. So I feel nothing but affection for those wealthy people who choose from everything in the world, the things I like.

Speaking for myself, I would acquire everything I liked, if I could acquire them without holding a steady job, while wearing boots, blue jeans, and a cut-off *Transformer* T-shirt. That was my rule when I was slimmer. I have worn a suit and tie once in my adult life, to a Picasso opening at MOMA. I walked in, and there was Nelson Rockefeller in boots and blue jeans. I walked up to the Rock and said, "Governor, could I have worn that tonight?" He said, "Absolutely, young man. This is America." I never wore a suit and tie again, and I cannot deny that collectors and dealers are very rough people, ruthless but sentimental, yet for all our arrogance and vices, we have always seen one another at our best.

In Holly Solomon's last years, when she was fragile and always in pain, she and her son Thomas would come to Las Vegas every few months. Holly was no longer the glamour girl of her Warhol portrait but she still had the flame. She always wanted to visit artists' studios. There were wild-girl artists in Vegas then, and in a very touching way, Holly would counsel them about the dangers and benefits of that condition, one wild girl to another.

Late in the 1960s, the Dallas collector Betty Blake gave a party for the artist Jim Roche. When I honked in front of Jim's hovel, he came out barefoot in cut-off jeans. Cut-offs okay, but barefoot after 6pm in North Dallas is a problem, so I had to make a decision because I was Jim's dealer. When we arrived at Betty's, while the puzzled valet guy looked on, I pulled off my boots and socks and we presented ourselves as barefoot boys at Betty's front door. She laughed out loud and suggested that we wander into the living room, admire her new Alfred Jensen, and scrunch our toes in the carpet.

Dominique de Menil, the queen of the Houston art world, was not as much fun as Betty. The first time I met La De Menil, she had on an exquisite Givenchy suit; she was carrying a large, elegant handbag. She had come from a tea where she talked about art. As if to prove this, she reached into her purse and pulled out a more-than-priceless Cycladic funerary object. She handed it to me. She had passed this treasure around at the tea, presuming that art, like grace, could be communicated by touch. Since my hand was galvanized and shaking, I decided she might be right. Art wise, Dominique was a bit of a dog-in-the-manger, but a force to be reckoned with.

In the early 70s, I saw this exclamation scrawled on a redbrick wall in SoHo: "God Bless Sidney Lewis!" A month later, I walked into DeWain Valentine's studio in Venice Beach. Standing against the wall beside a rust-stained sink and an antique stove was the Starship Enterprise of all refrigerators, gleaming like the Utopian future. Over the next few years, I came upon spanking new washer-dryers, big-screen televisions, and kitchen ranges in gloomy storefronts and blasted lofts inhabited by starving artists. This was because, in addition to their high-end collecting, Sydney and Frances Lewis from Richmond, Virginia, owned Best Products, and they liked to send their appliance catalogues to struggling young artists who could trade a work of art for anything in the catalogue. It's impossible to explain today the abject gratitude they garnered or how much innocent pleasure Sydney and Frances seemed to take from playing Santa.

In the same vein, I must confess here that Stanley and Elyse Grinstein in Los Angeles have fed me more often than my mother ever did. Instinctively understanding the panic I felt in Acapulco, Stanley has picked up the check at nearly every after-opening restaurant gathering I have attended in Los Angeles over the last twenty-five years. The Grinsteins have also purchased the first work of art that most of my friends ever sold. They have snatched artists back from the brink of oblivion with a graciousness that dissolves all shame. In the late 60s and early 70s, Stanley and Elyse kept an open account at an art store and a lumberyard so the young artists they had befriended could acquire materials, no charge, no strings, and, believe it or not, artists actually vied with one another in their efforts not to abuse this generosity. Today, I figure, that lumber and paint is worth a few billion dollars.

In the late 80s, I gave a talk at a Chicago penthouse wall-papered with Chias and Cucchis. After my talk, I took questions. The smug curator who had invited me solicited my opinion about the art on the walls. This seemed both gauche and malicious, but I am not a sissy. I just shrugged and said, "Starter art." This concluded the questions. I stood there for a long moment, feeling very lonely, until a man walked over and introduced himself as Lew Manilow. He introduced me to his wife, Susan. Then he put his arm around my shoulder and took me around the room, introducing me to every cowed guest, and I knew that I had met one of the better dudes in the world. The next day, the Manilows had me over for lunch. We did what I like best. We sat in a quiet room and talked about the Kiefers and the Richters on the walls, about the Richard Serra out in the garden. Not starter art, for sure.

I live in Santa Fe now, but I lived in Las Vegas for twenty years, and I had collectors to talk with about art. It goes without saying that they don't respect your judgment. (Otherwise Steve Wynn would have a great Cy Twombly, although he does have Steve Martin's Lichtenstein, with the frame. To their credit, these guys don't call their friends for social approval. They just buy it with a check, and screw you if you don't like it. So I have pals like Steve

Wynn, Glenn Schaeffer, Roger Thomas, Lee Cagley, Lorenzo Fertitta, Robin and Danny Greenspun, and Steve Molasky in Vegas and we can talk with about art. They are all richer than sin, so we don't hang out except at galas, but they call Libby and I to come over and see their new Damien Hirst, Howard Hodgkin, Joan Mitchell, Julian Schnabel, Vermeer, Larry Bell, Roy Lichtenstein, Mary Heilmann, or Vija Celmins. We talk art about art, not money. This is unusual, and, over the years, obviously, I have given some thought to this mysterious pastime. I have wondered about its social relevance, and decided that it teaches people with power and money to exercise subtlety and generosity in their decision making. I have also learned that there is no good reason for me to disdain fellow citizens who like what I like. I like people who do what I would do—if I could do it in a *Transformer* T-shirt.

Stupid Money

BACK in the 1970s, I was living in Nashville playing music and writing songs. Once a week, Billy Joe Shaver and I would trudge around Music Row together, pitching our songs to record producers. Billy was showing me the ropes, and he sold ten songs for every one I sold. I told him that, obviously, he was ten times better than I was. Billy said he was only five times better, and that quality had nothing to do with selling songs. This was business, Billy said.

"I could take yourn and sell 'em," he said. "You could take mine and not sell a one. You couldn't sell them because you don't look at the toes of your boots in the presence of their greatness. You couldn't sell them because I have three missing fingers from a sawmill accident, and you have a brownstone on East 50th Street. You couldn't sell them because I quit junior high school to join the Navy. You can read French, Spanish, and music. If you want to know what's a good song, ask Waylon Jennings or Bobby Bare. The rest of these jerk-offs only know that helping Dave doesn't make them feel good, and helping Billy Joe makes 'em feel great—like feeding a tramp at the door."

Billy Joe proved to be right. Except for Waylon Jennings and Bobby Bare, all the songs I sold in Nashville, I sold to college graduates [not a large community]. At the same time, I was right too. Billy Joe was ten times better than I was, and he didn't need Michel Foucault to tell him that patronage is invariably driven by inadequacies of the patron. So even if you win, you lose, because the buyer still doesn't know what they've bought. I asked Billy Joe if it bothered him, conning hillbillies into buying songs.

"It's all stupid money," Billy Joe said. "Here endeth the reading."

This raises a question for struggling artists today: If blood money leaves blood on your hands, if dirty money soils everything it touches, what does stupid money do to you and your art? This is the artist's dilemma at this moment. There's money out there but it doesn't mean anything. And the adventure started out so brilliantly in the aftermath of World War II. An assortment of confident, tough-minded, thick-skinned Americans, working in down-market lofts in downtown Manhattan, began putting together a contemporary art scene. Everyone who discovered this project tried to kill it and failed.

In the face of philistine ignorance, academic disdain, media contempt, and public anxiety, these unofficial masters created an art world. It was not a particularly big art world or a particularly rich one, but it was enough of an art world to claim a victory over rectitude. It was enough of an art world that the fearful powers-that-be set out to colonize what they had only recently failed to kill. Representatives of the government, the academy, and the press began venturing below 14th Street, poking around in dingy lofts, looking for their "fiddle in the middle," as we say in Vegas. A year or so later, they claimed this new art world as their own invention, citing the fantasy of American exceptionalism.

They proclaimed the triumph of American art to everyone from the ACLU, to the CIA, to the CIO, to Time Inc. They all bit off a piece of American Style Painting. They gobbled up Pop and Minimalism in one gulp. Everybody forgot that American institutions are designed for average American citizens and should stay out of the quality business. European institutions privilege the elite, the wealthy, and the brilliant. America is a statistical democracy. It's about the averages and the mean. It only concerns itself with quality for business reasons. We privilege the guy in the middle of the shopping mall cursing, and poking at his iPhone.

This is the emblem of our glory—a testament to the wisdom of our Founders who understood that brilliant Americans could figure things out, while the guy poking at his iPhone needed help. They also recognized genius as a genetic accident, a diamond in a coal pile. Madison habitually reminded his colleagues that mediocrity is a fact, so it is best to plan for it and increase the percentage of handicapped parking zones. None of these statutory conditions mean that Americans can't produce great art, literature, and music. It's just harder to do because American institutions are adversarial, not hierarchal. They level things out and thank god for that. The government thinks "normal." In their view, confidence is always over confidence. Courage is always foolish courage, and beauty is always too beautiful.

Confidence, courage, and beauty are not average and, therefore, beyond their bureaucratic purview. So postwar American art was not a *celebration* of America. It was a *cure* for America! To be an American is to be trapped like a fly in a web of relentlessly disembodied and admirably intentioned categories. American art in the wake of World War II was a cure for all this, a refuge from statistics, arbitration, legislation, checks, and balances, legislated fairness, administration, accounting, sociology, theology, psychology, and all of their evil kin. So if you wanted to achieve some awareness of yourself as an actual, sentient, physical creature in the atmospheric world, you needed to stand in front of a riotous Jackson Pollock, a glistening Donald Judd, or a tough, crusty, fundamental American flag painted by Jasper Johns and salute, and talk to your children about it as you would talk about a ball game.

This first dominant American art world, we must remember, was about dominant objects that rescued us from statistical oblivion. Dominant objects, however, don't vote or pay taxes. They don't pay tuition or do research. They are *sui generis* and, as such, statistically opaque. They don't get drunk and piss in your fireplace or hire impostors to give their lectures. So the hucksters picked away at the edges of this new art world as if it were a scab, and a new consensus arose: We should forget about vulgar objects and focus on *people*. That would be the *American* way. People eat, shop, vote, and pay tuition. Meanwhile, experts kept telling administrative poo-bahs that this was the magic moment; American art was in the lead and we needed a lot more American artists to maintain our lead in the "arts race."

We should educate these artists in universities and lavish them with the encouragement of losers, time servers, predators, and bureaucrats. They would "evolve" and "develop" as children do [and art does not], so upon graduation, they could form a community, like a Middle European village. They could stick together and support one another like urban pioneers. Thus it was that, around 1974, the "art world" became the "art community." People began having "potluck dinners" in SoHo, with the kids tumbling on the floor. The dark streets felt cozy. Middle-class shopping opportunities proliferated. Even though every one of these new ideas was wrong, stupid, and destructive to the creation of dominant objects. They triumphed anyway because they were mushy, sociological, American business ideas. I moved to Nashville to hang with Waylon, Willie and Billy Joe.

It was clear enough to me that the new ethos of inclusiveness posited a steady cash flow for the government, the academy, and the press. By focusing on *artists* rather than *art*, bureaucrats could deal with what they knew, and there would be photo opportunities. This meant more grants and fewer objects, more doctorates and fewer objects, more photos of beautiful people and fewer objects, more profiles in the newspaper and fewer reviews of exhibitions. We could encourage "creativity" because "creativity" is a business idea—actually, an obstetric idea—and not an art idea at all. Business gurus erroneously assured us that we were *all* creative, so why shouldn't we indiscriminately fund and cuddle any fool who wanted to become an artist?

Here, enumerated, are the reasons why we shouldn't have done this: First, quoting Justice Oliver Wendell Holmes, there is nothing so commonplace as the wish to be remarkable. Second, in the realm of genetics, the law of large numbers teaches us that nurturing a gazillion slide guitarists would not create one Duane Allman. Third, the pool of potential van Goghs in the United States is largely predetermined in primary and secondary schools where students who are bipolar, obsessive compulsive, hyperactive, narcoleptic, dyslexic, or morbidly obese are shunted through no fault of their own into "the arts" to keep the class grade averages up to legislated standards. Once "in the arts," these clinical refugees find themselves at a competitive disadvantage in a profession that makes great physical and social demands. One's *steadiness* in the studio and at the dinner table is a price point. Fourth, I have never seen a bad artist "evolve" into a good artist. Bad artists decide one morning that they don't want to make bad art anymore. They start making good art. I have seen this hundreds of times.

Reason five: Over the last decade I have spoken or consulted with the representatives of *thousands* of groups who "support the arts." I have spoken with local, state, national, and international organizations, associations, projects, groups, departments, endowments, foundations, alliances, and committees, and not once, in all this chatter [with the single exception of Ann Pasternak Slater] has any one of these people, even *mentioned a work of art* or given any sign of knowing what a work of art might be or where one might be found. This is cruel and elitist, but it is true. These "art professionals" are kind, generous well-intentioned C-students, and for them it's all about young artists, local artists, regional artists, international artists, ethnic artists, outsider artists, hundreds of thousands of artists, all equally deserving of care and support. They are the jolly nurses with plates of green Jell-O masquerading as "art professionals," and they are silly people with the money to bestow.

So if you are revolted by blood money and appalled by dirty money, what's your position on stupid money? And who grants the genius the stupid money? Nobody. We all know that it would be better for the "community" and less "controversial" to grant the gift to someone milder and more attractive rather than some talented, ferocious twit who might tear up the check in your face. Thus, talented and ferocious twits are discouraged by an art culture that is too stupid and tasteless to command any respect, and twits have choices. The most gifted twits I have met in the last decade have taken one look at what goes on in Chelsea and fled like wolves out on to the steppes because stupid money might help buy a spa but there is no honor in it and honor is what you want.

In my extensive experience, there is absolutely nothing to be done. All I can propose for "local artists" is that they buy a bus ticket out of town before they have another baby. Stupid money is not going to make you any smarter, any braver, help your prices, or give you confidence. It can only delude you while you piss away twenty years doing residencies and teaching in bad schools. It is the discourse that accrues around dominant objects, real or imaginary, that will survive us. Dominant objects will make subdominant objects shrivel like raisins. As David Hume observed, culture is about objects and institutions that survive their makers and the fecklessness of their patrons. The idiocy of American patronage, however, does not mitigate the fact that stupid money is real money, but so is the money you make selling crack or fracking. As any collector will tell you, dominant objects are a *cure* for money. Here endeth the reading.

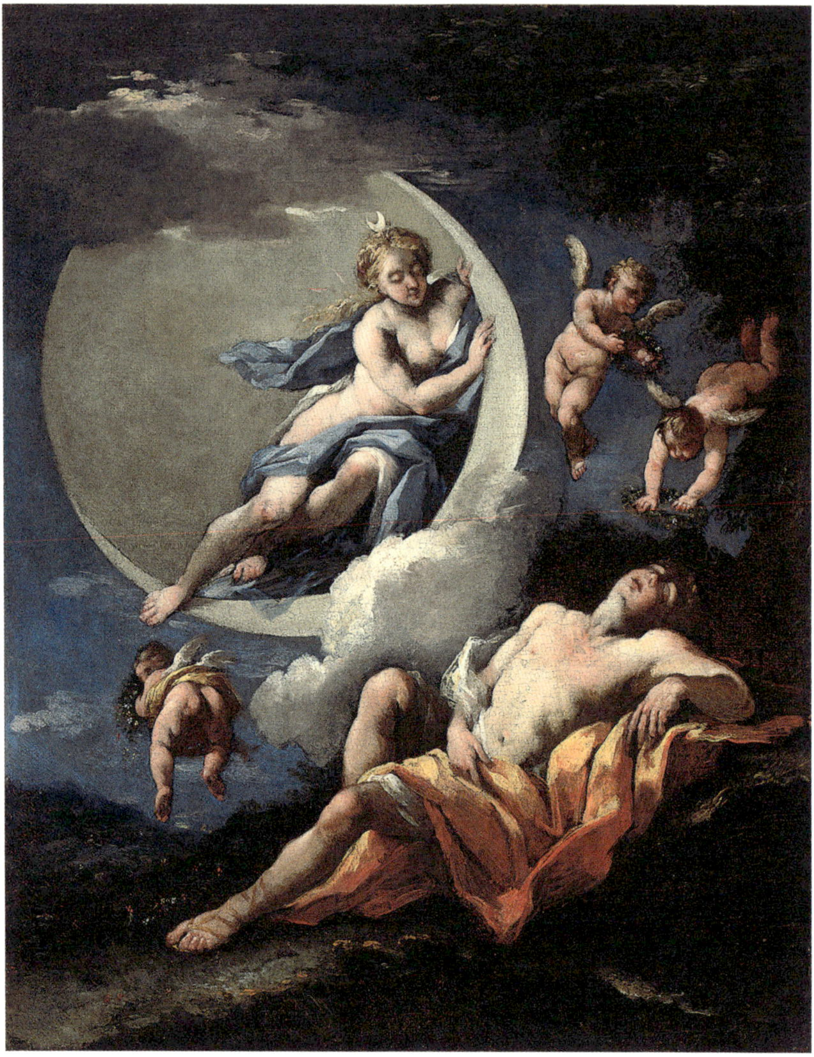

Michele Rocca (Parmigianino)
Diana and Endymion, 1751
Oil on canvas
55.5 × 44.8 cm | 21⅞ × 17⅝ in

Some Things Are Better than Others

It's no fun stumbling around in the twilight of one's own relevance, but it's doable and, occasionally, satisfying. I look around every day and thank the gods of art that no piece of art criticism written by me or anyone else has contributed a single whiff of pheromone to the fragrant panache that has sustained the art world as a market in luxury goods for nearly two decades. All you need is Page Six, fashion ink, the esteem of the investment bankers, and a passing familiarity with comic books. These will maintain your Ferraris, ugly paintings, and boring videos as objects of status and delectation. Since your Ferraris are not likely to be honored by a museum exhibition, a super gala, and a photo spread in *Town and Country*, your luxury art is all the more attractive as a social instrumentality, especially when you factor in the elevated levels of self-esteem derived from swanning around Sotheby's waving your little paddle.

During art's tenure as a luxury commodity, however, economic problems have arisen. First, everything is customized and nothing is new. Second, the vestigial infrastructure of arbiters, who once sought to convince us that the value of art transcends its luxury status, still exists; it just doesn't arbitrate, because nonindentured writers like myself are too expensive, and professors will write free to get themselves tenure, and, needless to say, daring value judgments will not win you the affection of the old farts who you hope will grant you tenure. So writers and talkers like myself, who would rather be right than rich, are out of the value game. If magazine reviews are not positive or completely opaque, advertising executives will not allow them, lest they lose a full-page ad.

The Chinese wall that divided advertising from editorial when I edited *Art in America* has disappeared completely. Advertisers can suppress coverage. They can even *buy* coverage with a four-color back-cover ad, a nice lunch, and a little schmooze. When I was a young art dealer, Leo Castelli, the Janis brothers, and Irving Blum were my mentors. They believed a dealer's job was to build great collections and create a market in which price and value maintained some magnetic attraction, so, in an ideal world, things cost what they were worth. That's gone forever, so maybe we aesthetes were wrong, or maybe we were right in our theory but wrong in our taste. Maybe everything we liked was crap, and art is nothing but decorative fodder that costs too much or too little, depending on your disposable income.

The art market, as a market in art, can no more tolerate this situation than critics can. The dealers are finally facing the cold consequences of banishing the only cure for art's deficiency as a luxury product. Unlike precious stones, rare metal, and *Fabergé cloisonné*, works of art have no intrinsic value. You can't break art down like a vintage Jaguar and sell it for parts, with the exception of Damien Hirst's diamond skull. All of art's value is extrinsic. As a result, back in the twentieth century, art made with silver, gold, or diamonds was relegated to the status of "decorative art," but no more, of course.

Back in that day, serious players invested art with value in public. Critics with dazzling track records, like Leo Steinberg, were willing to put their reputations on the line, take chances, and make public bets on the value and longevity of problematic artworks. This coterie of arbiters included gallerists, collectors, critics, scholars, magazine editors, auction houses, curators, and acquisition committees. Today the bulk of disinterested arbiters has been bought off or priced out of the market. The ongoing public quarrel about "quality" raged for nearly a century between collectors, critics, journalists, activists, publishers, dealers, curators, and scholars, and it generated a fairly stable constellation of relative value among players on the field; it served a vital economic function for artists during their uneasy transition from "young artist" to "midcareer artist." This is a dangerous passage, and nonfiduciary investments can sustain objects in public notice while the hungry spotlight is roaming elsewhere.

For most of the twentieth century, this intellectual infrastructure was integral to the art market—as important as Moody's, Standard & Poor, the *Wall Street Journal*, the *Financial Times*, and CNBC were valuable to financial markets. Now these arbiters have fallen into disgrace, as well. Every market needs honest brokers with a stake in being right. There are generations of artists for whom a consensus of professional respect could carry them through times of no money better than money could carry them through times of no respect. A few museum shows and a nice essay during a lull meant that your prices would still be there when the spotlight came swooping back.

Among artists of my acquaintance, Ellsworth Kelly, Bruce Nauman, and Ed Ruscha have had moments of eclipse. John Baldessari, Jules Olitski, and Jo Baer, through no fault of their own, have suffered through moments out of the light. A nonpecuniary consensus of esteem among honest professionals carried them all through the valley of the shadow. Gossip and slick magazine ink doesn't offer the same fallback support when the sales curves dip. There are artists out there now who came into public vogue in the mid-1980s, after honest judgment, in all its cruelty, was suppressed. They are still wondering where the help was when they needed it. Numerous contemporary luminaries will soon be wondering the same thing.

So where *are* those critical squabblers whose interests and enthusiasms were purportedly immune to fashion? Well, first, they may have been wrong, realized they were wrong, and quit. I have never been wrong so I don't know how this feels, but by the late 80s a great many of my talented colleagues had died of AIDS, or (like actors leaving rehab) had "moved on." They were consulting for big corporations, curating in Idaho, and driving Audis. Once, in the 90s, a magazine editor asked if I would write a piece about David Salle's retrospective in Sweden.

Having no disqualifying opinion about Salle, I said sure, that it sounded like fun. Then the editor asked, "Well, do you want to do the 'pro' or the 'con'?" So there it was: the editor of a major art magazine that for twenty-five years had been an elite arbiter of international taste, whose covers I used to pushpin to the wall above my desk in graduate school, was abdicating its traditional power. The editor was withholding any appearance of the magazine's tacit support for either David Salle's art or my opinion for fear of damaging its precious advertising revenue. With this phrase, a publication that had once prided itself in being *right* opted for being *fair*, and fair, as we all know, happens once a year, and usually in the country.

After this, opinionated criticism became a weekend opportunity to play a few sets of argumentative badminton with Jeremy, Chris, Elaine, or Yve-Alain. Since an art magazine's imprimatur now meant nothing, and editors worked for the ad salesmen, and dealers ran department stores, many writers fell back on writing exhibition catalogues. This kind of writing is like scoring a movie: you just play along with the pictures and bring up the cellos here and there. It gains you no honor or secular readership, just scholarly footnotes, but it does provide an opportunity to write about art that you respect.

By the time the new MOMA building opened its doors, this new penchant for holding one's job by withholding one's commitment had so metastasized that the *New York Times* magazine ran no less than *seven* reviews of MOMA's new architectural barn—a lot of paper wasted to cover their glossy, marble butts. The excuse for this SoHo-style poster-papering was "fairness." In its name, dealers mimicked Bloomingdale's, and diversified their offerings to disguise their personal taste. They eroded their better judgment in the name of diversity and abandoned the single attribute that sustained Leo Castelli, Sidney Janis, Pierre Matisse, Leslie Waddington, and André Emmerich for thirty years: their eyes and ears. Art magazines fell back on printed interviews, advance blurbs, diversity centerfolds, and writers from Belgium. They followed works of art to Bali and Cairo as if they were supermodels to be photographed biennially in exotic settings. Scholarly typing awash with qualifying adverbs began passing for exhibition reviews. American academics declared their "academic" disinterest in finance and refused to inquire about the manipulation of the numbers.

This epidemic of fatal lunacy allowed predatory sociologists to demote the adult practice of visual art into the doggy puddle of "visual culture" wherein students might evade the mysteries of Blinky Palermo by wondering in prose whether Wolverine is the most angst ridden of the X-Men. By the turn of the century, every American PhD in art history could identify the iconography of burgeoning mercantile capitalism in Titian's paintings. One in 500 could tell a Titian from a Tintoretto. The auction houses snapped up these odd ducks to co-opt their expertise.

At first, some of us were delighted. We got bargains. Occasionally, we could pass off a good work of art as a trendy object if it was shiny. Eventually, though, many of my friends and colleagues who knew good from bad stopped caring, and after a decade or so of not caring, they didn't know anymore, and, for a professional in the arts, an inability to tell good art from bad is a terminal condition. This is no joke. Some works of art *are* demonstrably better than others, and, ultimately, it matters, because good art resists obsolescence and evaporation. If you look and see nothing, there's nothing there. It's elevator music, hospital furniture, AM radio. There is, in fact, so much of this high-priced confetti in Chelsea these days that the galleries who offer the best art at honest prices will almost certainly be the first to be undeservedly wiped out.

Part of what I am suggesting is that the art world is going through its own version of the Wall Street meltdown. When things were moving fast on the Street and oodles of money was being made, the complicated, time-consuming task of assessing the real value of complex financial instruments became an easy corner to cut, so it was cut. Then one morning, the markets opened and *nobody* knew what *anything* was worth. Those who *knew* they didn't know sold short and made a boodle of money, but the tandem magnetism between price and value evaporated anyway. In the art world today, auction houses play the same black-box function as the investment banks. Junk goes in. Gold comes out. Reserve prices are amazingly manufactured. Artworks are purportedly sold, and this could mean anything. Some are guaranteed; some are bought in; some are discreetly parked; and some have their prices run up by proxies, chandeliers, and phone phantoms. Short of outright espionage, there is no way of our knowing what sort of transaction has taken place.

No one has ever expected better of auction houses, however. They sell butter knives, for Christ's sake, snuffboxes and Jackie O's underwear. They matter now because they are the only players in the game speculating publicly on what art might be worth. It has been many years since I wrote the words: "This work is too expensive," and it will be years before I do again. If a work of art sells for ten times the price of another, we damn well ought to know why. If one Eric Fischl is worth ten John McLaughlins, something is askew, and there are no more coteries of opinionated lunatics arguing with coteries of entrenched fogies. There are no academic wise men, no censorious black intellectuals, bellicose Brits, thoughtful connoisseurs, or crusading feminists on their high horses. There are no ignorant children proclaiming that crap is crap. No outrageous queens whose lightest touch turns muck to magic. No more insightful curmudgeons or legendary collectors known for having a "good eye."

This cacophony invented most of the value that still remains attached to art in the market. Now it's silent when it should be deafening, because the larger and more complex the quarrel, the cleaner the outcome, as James Suroweiki argues in *The Wisdom of Crowds*.[1] Today we have auction prices with the ontological status of Donald Duck, and my telephone has been ringing. For the first time in twenty years, old acquaintances are calling about that Olitski they bought to cover the earthquake crack, about their Matthew Barney with its exquisite vitrine, about their itty-bitty Richard Tuttle, and that Keith Tyson thingy, whatever it is. All I can say is, keep it if you like it. Dump it if you don't, and henceforth remember that *quality is quantity*.

The quality of an art object is directly proportional to the amount of "something" that a work of art gives to someone who belongs to an engaged constituency of interest. Quality is assessed by the raw volume of buzz it elicits from critics, scholars, collectors, dealers, consultants, curators, and decorators. All these arbiters expect different things from art in different measures, so the works of art that deliver the most stuff to the most constituencies, that sustain the most complex constituency of admirers for the longest time, are the very best ones. Period.

This means that there is no one you can trust, not even the trustworthy, so collectors need to buy what they love or become quick studies in the dynamics of power niches, and many collectors are. There are lots of niches. There is art that sells to social movers, art consultants, and movie stars. There is art, like the work of my pal Steve Prina, that is much beloved by the intellectual elite. There are "kunsthalle darlings" like my late friend Mike Kelley, and biennale darlings whom I shall not mention. Homoerotic snapshots for west Hollywood salons, and regional, sexual, and ethnic constituencies can be very specialized. Familiarity with this Balkan landscape means that you can buy a photograph by Robert Mapplethorpe with confidence because his vogue far exceeds his built-in homosexual constituency. You can buy sculptures by Kenneth Price or Josiah McElheny knowing that their reputations outstrip their standing as craftsmen. You can buy paintings by Ellsworth Kelly well assured that their public vogue transcends their mastery and exquisite design.

Otherwise, you're on your own. No one is in the business of being trustworthy anymore. No one is in the business of liking art either. So buy what you like. Learn when you're wrong, and remember this whole affair may be a fantasy. Personally I look at art and ask myself these quantifiable questions: How long will I remember this work and how long will other people remember it, since I might want to sell it? Does this work give me more than works that are similarly priced? Is it better than works that are similarly styled? Is it better than the blank white wall upon which it hangs? Do I love this work, and, if so, how long would I love it? How much will I think about it? How much would I miss it? How often does this work surprise me? How many words can I write about it? How much should I pay for it? How much would I sell it for? What would I trade it for? How many people agree with me? Who are they? How complex is the constellation of objects within which it resides? How deep is its historical resonance? How much does it mean, and does that meaning matter? These are some of the plus-minus attributes of "quality."

When I need to be subtle, I ask myself if this work of art is giving me something I like or simply refraining from giving me things that I hate? *This* is a difficult question. The allure of seeing a work of art that you don't hate is very seductive. I usually buy a small one and cross my fingers because you can't just stand by and watch. The invisible hand of the market is not the hand of God, nor the hand of an unemployed art gardener like myself. One needs friends and detractors to bend the discourse. We need to clean the stables or move next door. This will not happen because quality, as I conceive it, is hard, and it's easy to convince some suit that junk is a gem. So try believing that market prices are a true measure of art's value. If you can live with that, good fucking luck.

1 James Surowiecki, *The Wisdom of Crowds: Why the Many Are Smarter than the Few*, Anchor, New York, NY, 2004.

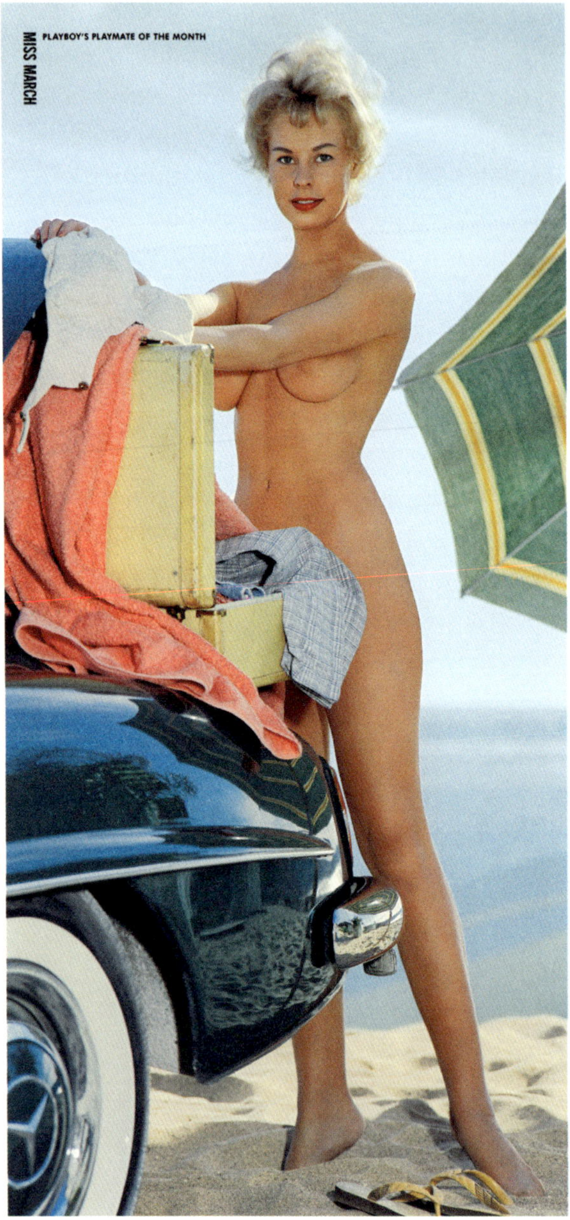

Audrey Daston, *Playboy* centerfold, March 1959

Playmates for Justice

MY FAVORITE anecdote from the Bush years concerns Attorney General John Ashcroft and the marble statue of blind Justice who stands naked in the lobby of the Department of Justice, with her blindfold and balance scales. The statue has adorned the lobby since the building's completion. Ashcroft, assuming his post, took one look and decided that naked Justice was too sexy for Americans and immediately commissioned an outsize toga to cover her classical boobs and buns, totally unaware that, in antiquity, the nakedness of Justice symbolized her innocence and transparency. Ashcroft's own aversion to innocence and transparency would soon become apparent, but without Hugh Hefner, I'm sure that Ashcroft would have presumed that Justice was purified by her marble classicism and walked right by. So, thank you, Hef, for outing Ashcroft's prudery and reinvesting our dream of justice with desire.

Nothing could be more American than this, according to my friend Heidi, who dances at the Crazy Horse Too in Las Vegas. When she is working, Heidi parades about provocatively naked. She will dance in your lap for money and, on the whole, she takes a homeopathic view of her profession. "There is no problem in the world," Heidi insists, "that cannot be solved by a roomful of naked women." I'd like to agree with her on this. Certainly, until very recently, excepting the Pashas, therapeutic roomfuls of naked women, have been in very short supply, and I think their effect on the difficulties encountered by Western Civilization could use a testing program. I'm lobbying to move Davos and the World Economic Forum to Las Vegas, but my hopes are not high since, until recently, even pictures of naked women were a rare commodity, unless those pictures had been gentrified and purified by the redeeming mantle of high culture in a big museum, which, of course, redeems pictures of naked women about as much as a lace peignoir. Here is Mark Twain's commentary, from *A Tramp Abroad*, on encountering a "gentrified" painting of a naked lady in a "purified" setting:

> You enter [the Uffizi], and proceed to that most-visited little gallery that exists in the world—the Tribune—and there, against the wall, without obstructing rag or leaf, you may look your fill upon the foulest, the vilest, the obscenest picture the world possesses—Titian's *Venus*. It isn't that she is naked and stretched out on a bed—no, it is the attitude of one of her arms and hand. If I ventured to describe that attitude, there would be a fine howl—but there the Venus lies, for anybody to gloat over that wants to—and there she has a right to lie, for she is a work of art, and Art has its privileges. I saw young girls stealing furtive glances at her; I saw young men gazing long and absorbedly at her; I saw aged, infirm men hang upon her charms with a pathetic interest. How I should like to describe her—just to see what a holy indignation I could stir up in the world.... yet the world is willing to let its son and its daughter and itself look at Titian's beast, but won't stand a description of it in words.... In truth, it is too strong for any place but a public Art gallery.

Twain's ironic point, aimed at his nineteenth-century audience, is that, as opposed to writing, one of the "privileges of gentrified art" was to be sexy—that the *Venus d'Urbino* (1538), even in the Uffizi, is still sexy, and that she hasn't always been a *Venus d'Urbino* or in the Uffizi. She is, in fact, the first and most famous Playmate, a picture of a naked woman whose erotic charge is willfully exacerbated by the fact that her body is idealized not by the rhetoric of classical art but, rather, by the rhetoric of Italian desire. She is a naked woman not an idealized nude. She came into being in the 1530s, when Guidobaldo della Rovere, heir to the Duchy of Urbino, borrowed some money from his mother to commission the painting from Titian. (Mothers, one presumes, were worldlier then.) When the painting arrived, Guidobaldo entered it in his catalogue of possessions as exactly what it was, not the *Venus d'Urbino* but a "picture of a naked woman." He installed this naked woman in his bedchamber where it hung like the Playboy Channel on digital hold.

Since mid-sixteenth century Italy, like mid-twentieth century America, was an age in which people were striving to shed their provincial roots and adopt sophisticated ways, the painting in Guidobaldo's bedchamber was not only acknowledged to be sexy, it was cool, too, and cosmopolitan, having come the entire 200 miles from Venice to Urbino. So, Guidobaldo's naked lady became a status symbol. So much so that Pope Paul III, sent his nuncio from Rome to Venice to commission his own naked lady from Titian. The Pope's only caveat was that his "naked lady" must be sexier than Guidobaldo's. A few months later, crazy with anticipation, Paul III sent his nuncio to Venice again just to make sure that the painting in progress was, in fact, sexier. The nuncio wrote back enthusiastically to reassure the Pope that *his* naked woman made Guidobaldo's naked woman look "like a frigid nun."

Unfortunately, we can't confirm the nuncio's judgment, since the location of the Pope's naked woman is presently unknown [which is to say, it's in the basement at the Vatican] but we can imagine the process that went into creating it, since Titian and his clients were liberating the erotic from Greek influence and redefining sexy in their own Italian language of desire, and this is a version of what Hugh Hefner was doing in the 1950s with *Playboy* magazine. He was inventing an American language of the erotic and distinguishing it from European habits, so the nuncio's consultation with Titian could not have been much different from Hefner's correspondence with Russ Meyer about Meyer's Playmate centerfold of his wife, the beautiful and bountiful Eve. Hefner's letter of March 1, 1955, goes like this:

> I'd like you to shoot this in front of the fireplace as before; let's get as big a fire in the fireplace as possible—the color of the flames is very welcome.
>
> Layout 1 is our first choice, with layout 2 a variation.... Let's use the same negligee and dangling earrings. Let's get rid of the cushions—they get in the way. Let's give Eve high heels. Let's give her, too, a champagne glass and place another before her as indicated. Thus we have already added a sophisticated element to our picture—a situation is suggested, the presence of someone not in the picture, so we've transformed a straight pin-up into an intimate interlude, something personal and special.
>
> Let's get the full figure into the picture. Try to come as close to the composition suggested in the layout as possible. It was set up, of course, especially for our double-page size.
>
> In costume, pull the negligee off the right shoulder to the elbow. Let the model rest on her left elbow. Model is a holding glass in her right hand. Let her cover her breasts with her right arm—let's hold this arm against the breasts, pushing them up against her in a more appealing shape.
>
> Let's try to keep the facial expression provocative but just a little less forced that we have here.

> As far as nudity is concerned, the barest suggestion of nipple is sufficient. Most of the shots submitted are very satisfactory in that respect.

It seems clear to me that Titian and Meyer, the Pope and Hefner are engaged in similar projects here, since Hefner's letter manifests a perfect Renaissance blend of erotic preference, class aspiration, aesthetic concern, and formal consciousness—a blend so perfect that these concerns are indistinguishable. The Pope wants a more intimate Italian style unsullied by Greek influences. Hefner wants an American erotic untainted by the neurotic signatures of its twentieth-century European counterpart. So there is no inference of dominance or submission, no "Mrs. Robinson" aura of transgressing age boundaries, no "Lady Chatterley" ambience of transgressing class boundaries, no appeals to cultural exoticism, like Gérôme's slave market, and none of the voyeuristic bang we get from late-Victorian soft-core, whose frisson derives from peeking in on naked women who are sleeping or otherwise unaware of our peeking presence. In Hefner's world, the girls look us in the eye and nothing changes but fashion and the seasons. In Hefner's universe, we are all bourgeois Americans. Some of us have better stuff and cuter girls. A charmed few [read Hefner] have ready access to roomfuls of naked women. The only mildly neurotic aspect of Hefner's eroticism, in fact, resides in his replacing the European binary of "playboy" and "courtesan" with Playboy and Playmate, which has a slightly queasy, preadolescent buzz to it, although I am happy to attribute this to the innocence of Hefner's belief in the Edenic promise of sophisticated cosmopolitanism.

So the Hefner Effect is about naked women. It is always about naked women, but it's not *all* about naked women, and we should never attribute this interest in naked women with the least whiff of vulgarity. In Hefner's universe, from the very beginning, pictures of naked, perky, good-hearted babes were there to *rescue* us from vulgarity, to make us real Americans in the aftermath of World War II, when nobody knew for sure just what a real American was. Not everybody who came home from the war went home to the farm and the hamlet. People returned to the cities and to the coasts. They began new lives in places where mom and dad were no longer available over the back fence or down at the hardware store for advice on life and living, cooking and gardening, decorating, and fixing the car.

In response to this diaspora, the American mass media began to function *in loco parentis*, doing the jobs that mom and dad would have done if they weren't back in Kansas and so resolutely old-fashioned. In their absence, recipes were printed on the box or on the can. For tips about the house and garden, there was *House and Garden*; for women's clothing, there was a social ladder of magazines escalating from *Charm* to *Vogue,* which Mary McCarthy charts in an exquisitely feline essay; for tips on entertaining there was the *Ladies' Home Journal*; for odd jobs, there was *Popular Mechanics*; and for guidance on being a normal American, there was *The Saturday Evening Post*. Finally, for paternal insights into time and life, there were, of course, *Time* and *Life*.

Hefner, mostly in aid of his own education, introduced a new character into this nuclear media family. I call him Uncle Reggie. He is the male equivalent of Auntie Mame, who has a movie but doesn't have a magazine, unless you count Helen Gurley Brown's *Cosmopolitan*. Uncle Reggie does something vague in the city, but he drops by from time to time to sit in the living room with his legs crossed, in his designer duds, smoking a long cigarette, and surveying the furniture with mild disdain. Uncle Reggie tells you about the grand restaurants and chic nightclubs in New York, Chicago and LA. He chats about fast cars, hi-fi, fashion models, cool black musicians, and the great artists he's met, disheveled in their tuxedos. He shows you a world that is naughty and sleek but still pretty nice, still quintessentially American and nothing like the decadent world of those Euro-trash *bon vivants* for whom the term *playboy* was invented.

Through the vehicle of his magazine, Hefner became everybody's Uncle Reggie. He showed up in the mailbox and on the newsstands every month [behind the counter in Kansas, with the rubbers]. The most ravishing gift he brought us with his magazine is beyond calculation, and it had nothing to do with the cosmopolitan accoutrements he advertised. Even today, there is no real way of assessing the profundity of *Playboy*'s impact, but here is the fact: When Uncle Reggie arrived, he brought his sensibility into the neighborhood. In effect, he stood on the porch, waving his cigarette, and took note of Sally Ann, who was watering the lawn next door. "Very nice boobs, don't you think?" Uncle Reggie would say, granting you permission to gawk at the boobs you had been gawking at anyway, but not like an animal, not like a redneck, like a cosmopolitan man of the world, a connoisseur of fine women, fine wine, and Ornette Coleman.

Like many a visionary before him, Hefner aspired to civilize the savages. In the process, he established himself as the Norman Rockwell of American sex. He eroticized the neighborhood. He not only transformed awkward adolescents into aspiring playboys [civilizing them just a little], he transformed the cheerleader next door into a potential playmate, a pneumatic Aphrodite with her own desires and cosmopolitan aspirations, who might come over one afternoon and dig some cool tunes. Simply put, Hefner stripped small-town sexuality of Protestant angst and Catholic anguish. He instituted what can only be called a velvet revolution, based less on ideas about having a lot of sex than on a pervading vision of the sweetness and the grandeur of ordinary American life—enhanced by having a lot of sex. As a philosopher-professor friend of mine once remarked, "The Playboy Philosophy is not a *great* philosophy but it's a not bad one."

A woman friend of mine, who now teaches women's studies in the Ivy League, credits Hefner with civilizing the teenagers she dated in high school, for mitigating their feral aggression with a patina of cool. The Pop artist Tom Wesselmann, in homage to Hefner, began painting a grand series of stylized odalisques titled "Great American Nude" [begun in 1961.] The funny, serious joke in the title of Wesselmann's "Great American Nude" is that *there are no* "great american nudes" in the history of American art, unless you count the naked boys in Thomas Eakins's *The Swimming Hole* [1884–85]. Unlike the art history of Europe, which abounds with naked women and where, *quelle surprise*, Wesselmann sold most of his paintings, the art history of America is chaste, domestic, and mostly about trees and real estate. Throughout the history of painting in the American republic, the painting of naked women has been suppressed on whatever principle falls to hand.

There has always been somebody in goal to protect us from images of naked women. Puritans, transcendentalists, regionalists, radicals, expressionists, minimalists, feminists, academic materialists, and postcolonialists—not to mention the ghost of Martin Luther—all have served their time in the net. And all it took to blow away the cobwebs in the age of T. S. Eliot, Irving Howe, and Lionel Trilling was a Midwestern dude with a magazine, who reminded us of what we already knew: that a rose is a rose is a rose, is a rose—is eros itself, omnipresent and omnipotent, who reminded us that the ravishing surfaces of the world are as beguiling as the so-called content these surfaces conceal. In the process, Hefner not only made sex zipless, he legitimized and elevated a brand of art that was hitherto beyond the pale.

The tradition of American art, and of American photography in particular, has always presumed that the artist is personally disengaged from his or her subject, disinterested in its physical appeal and beyond its power. American artists were interested in news value and elegant form. They were not pornographers, and, even when they were, we were expected to look at Minor White's beautiful boys and think, "Oh, what an elegant curve"—this was the argument lawyers raised in defense of Robert Mapplethorpe's blatant pornography in an Ohio courtroom. The American photographer was presumed to be "our guy" looking at the world for us and pointing things out. Erotic photographers, however, are engaged with their subjects, not with us. They can only make it sexy for themselves. If we respond, we do so through their eyes, looking in on the intimate relationship between artist and his or her subject, and some of the best Playmate photographers were women, like Bunny Yeager and Suze Randall. Hefner said, "Hey, why not? New eyes can't hurt, and we like women around here."

Thanks to Hefner, then, 200 years of people admiring the butt of a marble lady at the Justice department have come to an end. Today, the aesthetic/erotic bang of work by artists like Robert Mapplethorpe, Nan Goldin, John Currin, and Lisa Yuskavage derive from an erotic engagement of artist and model that has its roots in Hefner's revolution. The whole *point* of Mapplethorpe's photographs is that guys turn him on. The same bodies and acts photographed "disinterestedly" die on the page. Mapplethorpe's complicity invests his pictures with a chilly heart. It makes them radical, personal, and not a little dangerous. All Hefner did was confront the gap between what we are told and what we know—then come down on the side of what we know—that only madmen are disinterested.

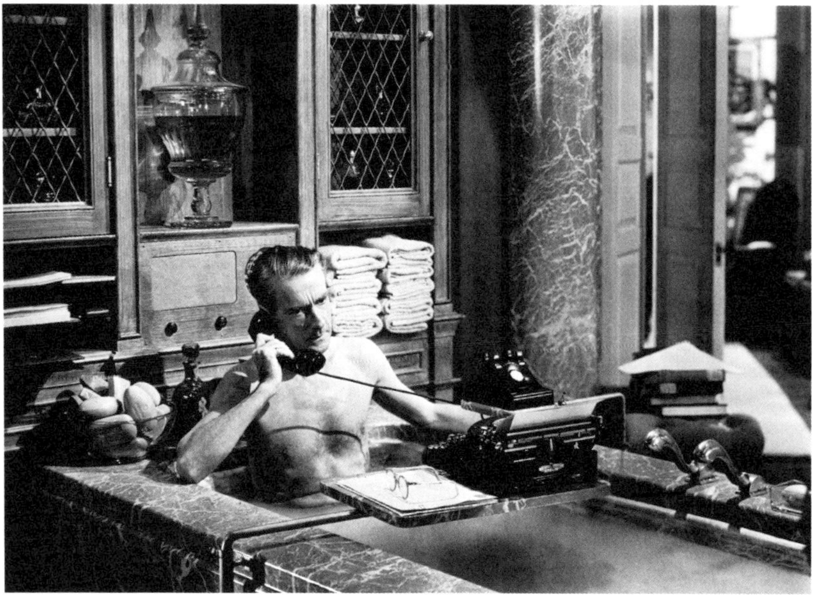

Clifton Webb as Waldo Lydecker in *Laura*, 1944
Film still

Waldo, Two Wilsons, and Joe

I AM one of those people who would topple consciousness from its throne. In my acid-stained youth, I toppled it as often as I could. Since then I have been drifting down this long, white corridor, past a million miles of art, snatching words like bubbles out of the blue. I do not repudiate consciousness. It's useful for doing your taxes and ordering pizza, but I discovered early on that I am less beguiled by the tedium of consciousness than by its invisible colleague, the unconscious. My own unconscious, which knows me like a good valet, does things without being told. It does most of my thinking for me these days. I just let things float until they find their proper places. I use my conscious awareness for writing, of course, but not exclusively. While I'm thinking away and struggling hard for *claritas*, I'm simultaneously floating on a swirl of word bubbles, waiting for *them* to find *their* places. That is literally the way it works, no poetry intended.

This essay is written in homage to Timothy D. Wilson's *Strangers to Ourselves: Discovering the Adaptive Unconscious*,[1] a modest book that helped me understand what I have been up to. Wilson's book gives the unconscious a cool-headed empirical upgrade that has been overdue for years. It supplants Freud's sweaty dog pit of repression with a beautiful design idea. The occasion for

Wilson's re-design is nothing major, just an ongoing professional quarrel about the two standard methods of personality testing. Some researchers believe that the human personality is best studied through self-reported personal narratives. Others swear by a filmed interview format that takes nonverbal factors into account. Both interpretive models are predictive of behavior, but when these two methods are used to assess the same person, they describe two different personalities.

Researchers quarrel about the right, or best, method. They wonder which personality might be the "authentic" one. Wilson applies Occam's razor to their argument. He proposes that *both* methods are right—that we are, indeed, two different people: We each have a conscious self with whom we are all too familiar and intimate, and an unconscious self unknown to us but all too familiar to our friends, enemies, colleagues, and confidants. So consider the elegance of Wilson's idea: He takes the two dead zones in our awareness—our purportedly "subterranean" selves and "ourselves as others see us"—and combines them. Our conscious self is cloistered in Wilson's model. Our unconscious self is not. Out of sight to us, our unconscious exists in plain sight of the world.

This, I think, explains all the couture, surgery, workouts, makeup, and perfume that we employ to reconfigure our outer selves to comply with our inner, conscious selves. And, when you think about it, it's not really that surprising that the two testing procedures would describe two personalities. The personal narrative methodology of personality testing is almost guaranteed to elicit agreeable, self-aware citizens who rationalize their actions and motives, soothe their adversaries and please their mothers. The interactive methodology that incorporates more physical observation, however, always elicits more social confirmation. It also describes a public self that we cannot recognize. Wilson identifies this rogue self as the "adaptive unconscious."

He proposes [and Freud would agree with him here] that this adaptive unconscious has its own personality. In Wilson's model, however, the "adaptive unconscious" thinks fast and does more work than we have hitherto attributed to it.

I can live with this. Twice in my teaching career I have been blessed with students who were inspired mimics. When they deftly "did" their classmates, I always laughed and knew just who was being "done." I became confused, however, when one of these impersonators stood up and did *il professore*. With the first goofy, careless explosion of cigarette ashes, everyone laughed, screamed, rolled on the floor, and clutched their tummies. I would be looking on in *utter* incomprehension, recognizing nothing, thinking maybe the kid is doing Joe Cocker. But what do I know? I look more than I am looked at, and my clunky Joe Cocker persona, the one who actually inhabits the world has become fuzzy around the edges. My conscious self-image is more like Waldo Lydecker, the effete art critic played by Clifton Webb in the film *Laura*. So if you tell me that I have two selves, fine. This means that my wife is right and Timothy Wilson is too. I have two personalities; each has its own ways, its own motives, and its own tasks. If you tell me that neither of these selves knows the other, because my adaptive unconscious is a black box in a puddle of tar, that seems right to me, too.

So I am me, but I am also this other guy, that I only glimpse in the widening eyes of shocked dinner companions and, occasionally, when surprised by a mirrored mirror in a hotel suite. My Waldo Lydecker conscious self doesn't recognize impersonations of my Joe Cocker unconscious self, and Joe, if the truth be told, is so reckless that he scares us both. Waldo is always pulling us back from the brink, murmuring apologies and explanations. This is tremulous Waldo's *job*! He cannot play the piano or dodge a piano falling from a window, but he can justify his inability to do so. First, Waldo is usually dozing. Second, he's too slow and too *thoughtful* for fast dancing or crisis management.

Waldo does one thing well: he rationalizes, which is the same thing as reasoning, I suspect. Like a bossy baby swaggering in its playpen, he convinces me that we're doing okay. He tidies things up and attempts to avoid anything that doesn't seem right. When all else fails, Waldo lies to me.

In Wilson's model, then, "consciousness" is no longer king, no longer the tip of the iceberg, as Freud would have had it, but something more like a small snowball atop a mighty iceberg. More specifically, consciousness is a package of new evolutionary software that we use when needed for spell-checking, book balancing, spin doctoring, pizza ordering, and long-range forecasting. My Joe Cocker-like adaptive unconscious is precedent and always on the job, automatically and instantaneously. Joe's job is to recognize patterns in the here and now, and, using emotional static, flag any entropy or irregularity or novelty for Waldo's attention. [Many of Freud's ideas about repression, I should note, become more elegantly explicable if they are considered precedent rather than subsequent.] Waldo could not survive an hour without Joe's guidance, but Joe has his own ways. There are things he likes, like T-Rex, and those he doesn't, like the Ring Cycle. Waldo, mostly, kvetches about Joe's vulgar taste, except for the band *Chic*. Waldo and Joe both like *Chic*.

This is why, when I am working, I find it best to tolerate as much craziness and static as I can and let Waldo sleep until he's really needed. His job is to be conscious when he needs to be. Like a lofty bureaucrat, he deals almost exclusively with reports and policy formation. On those few occasions when I am fully conscious, I am always arguing with my own precocious tastes and appetites. Introspection is about as much help as an executive wastebasket, because at the bottom of consciousness there is nothing but crumpled paper. The first-hand truths remain entangled with my unconscious Joe Cocker and the world that he reports to Waldo.

If we would know ourselves and the world beyond us, then, we must untangle the world from our instantaneous appraisal of it, like editors trying to divine the veracity of reportage from an unknown reporter named Joe. Absent psychedelics, and even with them, the adaptive unconscious is a free agent: It shows us what it will. But consciousness can learn and it can lie; it can imagine and pretend. We can emulate alternate states of consciousness and see the world "in character." By addressing the world from different angles, we can sometimes cleave the world from our imagination of it. Something like this happened on May 12, 1965, in the Stax recording studio in Memphis, Tennessee. Wilson Pickett was recording "In the Midnight Hour." Jerry Wexler was producing. The band was Steve Cropper, Al Jackson, and Donald "Duck" Dunn.

Wexler began the session out by emulating the way kids were dancing at that time, swinging their bodies around and thrusting one elbow back on the two beat and the four, so the emphasis didn't go "*boom* dah, *boom* dah," but something more like "um-*chaw*, um-*chaw*." The band began working out a rhythm track in this meter, with Pickett singing along. Later, listening to the replay, it sounded great, but not that great. Then, Pickett stepped up to the control board and pushed the fader on the snare drum way up, making the drum artificially loud as it fell emphatically on the two beat and the four. This made everybody dance, but it was worrisome. The replay sounded like a song but it didn't sound like a band, and in those days recording aspired to "hi-fidelity" to the original sound.

Somebody said, "The snare drum's too loud; it crosses the vocal." Pickett said, "They ain't *listening* to the snare. They listening to *me* while they dancing to the snare!" This remark created Lowell George's idea of "apparent volume" and changed the history of recorded music. Pickett insisted on keeping the loud, danceable snare drum, and Wexler released a record that, if you were expecting a band, sounded odd. No one noticed. They were too busy dancing. If you listen to the record today, the difference is not discernible, not after the Stones, Little Feat, and Fleetwood Mac. But something happened: Wilson Pickett abandoned his ego for a moment and listened to the song as an adolescent girl might listen, while dancing to a jukebox. By listening "in character," he *heard* what his adaptive unconscious was actually reporting. This rewrote the consciousness of everyone in the control room. Because they were dancing, the musicians became aware of their own self-delusion. They were *not*, in fact, making a picture of a band. They were making a *record*, and a *record* need not sound like a band! It only had to sound like music and make you *dance*!

After this, the word *hi-fidelity* disappeared. Recordings were no longer taken to have fidelity to something "real". They *were* something real. From this day forward, bands on stage strove to sound like the record. This maneuver, I should note, also marks turning points in the history of art. At the dawn of the Baroque, with the birth of Impressionism and with the ascendancy of Pop and Minimalism the "picture of the band" becomes a "record." Caravaggio, Monet, Warhol, and Judd do not represent the things that they depict. They reincarnate their subjects in an intensified reality. They take a step toward the threshold where the adaptive unconscious engages the world. This is why the tremulous Mr. Lydecker in my head—as vain and glib as he is—always defers to Mr. Cocker when he needs a little help from his friends, because the closer we get to the world, the crazier it gets.

1 Timothy D. Wilson, *Strangers to Ourselves: Discovering the Adaptive Unconscious*, Harvard University Press, Cambridge, MA, 2002

Beethoven Plays Music Row

I AM telling this story because music is the most self-sustaining of all the arts. It doesn't require an audience; it doesn't require fame, and it doesn't require some elevated brand of cultural respectability. You can sit in your room and play a Stevie Wonder song on your guitar—something like "All in Love is Fair," where the chords are altered by one note on every change, and it organizes your life. It makes you feel better. So this story is about my friends in Nashville who are session musicians and record producers. I would name them, but session players have Batman complexes. They love their secret identities. They have to be known to get work, but not that known. They know notorious guys. They know what it has done to them. Also, they would be embarrassed to be called "great musicians," although all of them are and know it.

Anyway, one afternoon after a session, a great, young bass player from Pensacola, who learned to play by moving the needle back and forth on the spinning vinyl, confessed to me that he had never seen a live performance of classical music. Over the next year, I expanded this posse of masters who had never seen classical music performed. When Vanderbilt announced that the symphony was opening a performance with Beethoven's "Ode to Joy," the fourth movement of his Ninth Symphony in

D minor, set to Schiller's poem, with chorale, I knew I'd found my venue, so I rounded up my posse of innocent savants. A few more knowledgeable musicians, like Elvis Presley's keyboard guy, tagged along too. [He taught composition at Vanderbilt.] I rounded up a lot of these guys and gals and forgot to prepare them for the fact that Nashville has a very snooty *beau monde*, and that the audience would be entirely attired in tuxes and gowns. We looked like an intramural basketball team, but we had great seats, and the local symphony is very good and very meticulous. [Nashville being Music City.] Also, a lot our friends were playing and singing on stage, and it was great for us to see members of our tribe, who spent their days "oohing" and "aahing" behind drunk hillbillies, standing out front, chunky and proud, blasting out "O Freunde, nicht diese Töne!"

It was great, and "Ode to Joy" was a perfect piece for nonclassical session players for a lot of reasons. The best "high-toned" reason comes [as it always does], from my hero, Glenn Gould, who argues, "It's precisely that impossible mixture of *naïveté* and sophistication that makes Beethoven the imponderable that he is. It's precisely ... the mixture of the professional's development skills and the amateur's motivic bluntness" that make Beethoven "the logical conclusion of the Western musical tradition." In his music "an elaborate exposé with which only a professional can cope is related to material with which anyone can identify."[1]

More critically in this case, nearly the whole of twentieth-century American pop music flows from the construction of this symphony, which is based on a mélange of repeated and dispersed motifs and leitmotifs. [This is what Gould means by "motivic"; we call them "lines" or "riffs."] The piece is alive with figures and obbligatos that never quite dominate and never quite disappear. Its main theme corresponds exactly to the base structure of a contemporary popular song. A thirty-two bar figure broken into four eight-bar phrases divided into Statement, Restatement, Release, and Return. Arranged in pop music, the structure is usually reframed by an extra verse or chorus in front and endless choruses at the end. So, you get Statement, Restatement, Release, Return extended at both ends for closure. There are a million variations on this structure, but that's all one needs to start. Also Beethoven's fourth movement is heroic and a little over the top—very pop in other words. It also has pulse and a pace. With a conductor who counts Presto at 185 beats per minute, as he should and ours did, the music moves right along. At this tempo, the piece lasts about twenty-one minutes, about seven times longer that the standard pop piece, although my colleagues translated the intervals easily.

This, if you'll forgive me, brings up a teaching point. Everybody plays Beethoven too slowly, in quest of solemnity, and everybody plays the Rolling Stones too fast in search of fun. In fact, most of "Ode to Joy" is played at 185 beats per minute; the Rolling Stones play "Tumbling Dice" at about 49 beats per minute. There is a tempo in this range between largo and adagio that rockers call the groove, and Charlie Watts (who has "slow down!" written on his snare drum) stays right in the pocket. Now, watch the feet of the tympani guys tapping away as they play Beethoven. Solemn pace doesn't mean serious; fast doesn't mean fun, as any woman can tell you. These infelicities arise from reading the music through a cultural bias, and most good musicians in any generation figure this out. Muscle memory is a genetic proclivity, so musical knowledge, riding knowledge, dancing knowledge, shooting knowledge, and oratorical skills evolve very slowly. In the history of Western music, the Ninth was yesterday.

So we sat there quietly through a bombastic, sort of Britpop intro. At ninety seconds, the first eight-bar statement of the theme is voiced and everybody took out their notebooks. A minute later, the Statement and Restatement are voiced, and then, about two and a half minutes in, the entire thirty-two-bar statement is introduced. It comes floating in very sotto voce, with cellos and bowed bass. This is the most satisfying introduction of a theme in all the music I know. Everybody started making notes at this moment. The second time through the theme, the chords are restacked, maybe up about a fifth, to make space for an oboe playing a loose figure in front of it. Somebody said, "Gerry Mulligan," and they were right. The theme kept repeating, gathering instruments like a parade, and everybody noticed when Beethoven started accelerating the pace by "jumping the one" in the Chorale, like James Brown, coming in on top of the beat at the first of a phrase. Art Pepper and Keith Richards do this, too.

When the vocals began, everybody noticed that the bass-baritone vocal line was supported from above. Flutes, piccolo, and strings held the shape of the harmony. In Nashville, vocals are always supported from below. This blurs out the low-end of baritone voices, like Waylon Jennings's and Johnny Cash's. [Later somebody noted that Jack Clement had recorded Waylon's voice using ride cymbals, a tambourine, and fiddle to support the vocals. This left the low end, melismatic blur of Waylon's voice free to be what it was.] After the first choral, Beethoven returns to the theme with the bass drum seeming to fall on the backbeat—like reggae or the blues. The notes feel like triplets, but they're not quite. In the Ninth, the illusionary back-beat and the jumped-one make for a very beguiling narrative of a theme we'd already heard plenty of—very New Orleans. Everybody loved this. Everyone liked the irresistible way they were compelled to ride the wave of the music as it rose and expanded.

Everybody seemed confused by the finale, and while we were standing around afterward on the Vanderbilt campus, where most of us had never been, although Vanderbilt is just across 19th Street from Music Row, nearly everyone mentioned the weirdness of the finale. I pointed out that Gould couldn't draw a bead on it either. Elvis's keyboard guy suggested that Beethoven was keeping formal promises that he had made in the first three movements that we hadn't heard that night—that he was tying everything up with a bow. After listening to the whole symphony, this seemed an astute observation, but it still doesn't work. Everybody got sound mixing ideas from Beethoven's fabulous diminuendos and crescendos. Everyone was gaga about the middle register. The unison cellos and the bowed bass were to die for. Stanley Clarke was evoked.

Several people mentioned that the music was less confident in the upper registers. Somebody remarked that Beethoven was deaf. In response, a producer said it was not about being deaf, it was about *going* deaf, as we all were. We listened at max volume all the time as a part of our jobs. The upper registers, above six kilocycles, are the first to go, and you start distrusting your judgment up there. Another producer suggested that the piece should be played today with the upper registers floating, and the alto obbligato bumped up, since the high end [much beloved as a sign of virtuosity in the nineteenth century] could no longer carry the tempo with any authority. We must have talked about an hour about music. Toward the end my young bass player friend was sniffling. "He never heard it," the kid said. "Yes, he did," someone else said, "except for the high end."

1 Glenn Gould, "Glenn Gould Interviews Himself about Beethoven," Tim Page [ed.], *The Glenn Gould Reader*, Random House, New York, NY, 1990.

Bibliographic References

Edited versions of these essays appeared in the following publications:

PIRATES AND FARMERS

Stardumb, art by John Defazio, Michael Mack [ed.], Artspace Books, San Francisco, CA, 2000.

THE WEATHER OUTSIDE

Tar Magazine, no.1, Fall 2008.

IDIOT

"Revision Number Nine: Idiot," *Art in America*, vol.97, no.2, February 2009.

COPING WITH PARADISE

"Coping with Paradise," *Peter Alexander: In This Light*, Orange County Museum of Art, Newport Beach, CA, 1999, and *Primary Atmospheres: Works from California 1960–70*, David Zwirner and Steidl, Göttingen, 2010.

ORPHANS IN THE STORM

"Revision Number Four: Orphans," *Art in America*, vol.97, no.1, January 2009.

VOGUE

"Revision Number Eleven," *Art in America*, vol.97, no.9, October 2009.

IN THE SUNSHINE OF ABSOLUTE NEGLECT

"In the Sunshine of Absolute Neglect," *Extreme Canvas 2: The Golden Age of Hand-Painted Movie Posters from Ghana*, Ernie Wolfe III [ed.], Kesho & Malaika Press, Los Angeles, CA, 2012.

FIRST WE FIGHT

"Fighting," *Octagon*, Brady Games, Indianapolis, IN, 2008.

FORMALISM

"Revision Number Seven: Formalism," *Art in America*, vol.97, no.4, April 2009.

FEAR AND LOATHING GOES TO HELL

"Sucking Pennies in the Seventies—Notes on the Good Old Daze and What Hunter Thompson Got Wrong," *Las Vegas Weekly*, February 15, 2007.

AMERICAN COOL

"American Cool," *Art Issues*, no.56, January–February 1999.

ON THE ROAD FOREVER

"On The Road Forever," *Las Vegas Weekly*, September 6, 2007.

NIGHTLIFE IN LA ZONA

"Dirty Pictures," *Boystown: La Zona de Tolerancia*, Aperture, New York, 2000.

NURTURING YOUR ADDICTIONS

"Revision Number Six: Addictions," *Art in America*, vol.97, no.3, March 2009.

LAS VEGAS FOR SISSIES

"Double or Quits," *Frieze*, no.50, January–February 2000.

BACKSTORY

"Revision Number Ten: Provenance," *Art in America*, vol.97, no.8, September 2009.

ART COLLECTORS

"Revision Number Three: Collectors," *Art in America*, vol.96, no.11, December 2008.

STUPID MONEY

"The God Ennui," Art Criticism and Writing Lecture Series, School of Visual Arts, NY, September 17.

SOME THINGS ARE BETTER THAN OTHERS

"Revision Number Five: Quality," *Art in America*, vol.97, no.2, February 2009.

PLAYMATES FOR JUSTICE

Playboy: Posters La Collection Complète, Editions de la Martinière, Paris, 2008.

WALDO, TWO WILSONS, AND JOE

"Revision Number Eight: Unconscious," *Art in America*, vol.97, no.5, May 2009.

BEETHOVEN PLAYS MUSIC ROW

First published in present volume.

Image credits

© Moviestore Collection/Rex Features: p.10.
© Everett Collection/Rex Features: p.16.
© Artisan/Everett Collection/Rex Features: p.22.
Photo: Jennifer Steinkamp, courtesy SITE Santa Fe, Santa Fe: p.37.
© 2013 Laddie John Dill, photo courtesy of the artist. Exhibited in 1971 in the exhibition *New Works for New Spaces* at Walker Art Center, Minneapolis. Purchased in 2010 for the collection of Museum of Modern Art, New York. Marguerite K. Stone Bequest [by exchange]. Photographer unknown: p.38.
Wreck of a Transport Ship, Turner, Joseph Mallord William [1775–1851]/ Museu Calouste Gulbenkian, Lisbon, Portugal/The Bridgeman Art Library: p.50.
Photo: Charlotte Southern. © Bloomberg/Getty Images: p.58.
Leonardo, b. 1960, Ghana. Courtesy Ernie Wolfe Gallery, Los Angeles: p.66.
Photo: Michael Ochs Archives/Stringer. © Getty Images: p.90.
Image from *Boystown* by unidentified photographer, courtesy of The Wittliff Collections, Alkek Library, Texas State University-San Marcos: p.112.
Photo © 2009 George Rose. © Getty Images: p.126.
© 2013. Image copyright The Metropolitan Museum of Art/Art Resource/ Scala, Florence: p.132.
Diana and Endymion [oil on canvas], Rocca, Michele [1666–1751]/ Private Collection/Photo © Christie's Images/The Bridgeman Art Library: p.154.
Courtesy PLAYBOY MAGAZINE: p.164.
Photo: John Kobal Foundation/Contributor. © Getty Images: p.174.
Photograph by Christine Taylor: inside flap.

Published in 2013 by Ridinghouse
5–8 Lower John Street
Golden Square
London W1F 9DR
United Kingdom
www.ridinghouse.co.uk

Distributed in the UK and Europe by
Cornerhouse
70 Oxford Street
Manchester M1 5NH
United Kingdom
www.cornerhouse.org

Distributed in the US by
RAM Publications
2525 Michigan Avenue Building A2
Santa Monica, CA, 90404
United States
www.rampub.com

British Library Cataloguing-in-Publication Data: a full catalogue record of this book is available from the British Library

ISBN 978 1 905464 40 1

Ridinghouse Publisher: Doro Globus
Edited by Karsten Schubert and Doro Globus
Editorial Assistant: Louisa Green
Copy-editor: Eileen Daly
Proof-reader: Karen Kelly
Intern: Mathilde Leblond

Designed and produced by Mark Thomson
Set in Gantoise and Macula
Printed in Italy by Studio Fasoli